THE HOLIDAYS

•

THE HOLIDAYS

*21 Menus
for
Elegant Entertaining
from
Thanksgiving
to
Twelfth Night*

•

JOHN HADAMUSCIN

•

*Photographs by
Marcia Luce*

Harmony Books/New York

Designed by Ken Sansone

•

Text copyright © 1986 by John Hadamuscin
Photographs copyright © 1986 by Marcia Luce

Published by Harmony Books, a division of Crown Publishers, Inc.,
201 East 50th Street, New York, New York 10022.
Member of the Crown Publishing Group.

HARMONY and colophon are trademarks of Crown Publishers, Inc.

Manufactured in the United States of America

•

Library of Congress Cataloging-in-Publication Data

Hadamuscin, John.
The holidays: 21 menus for elegant entertaining
from Thanksgiving to Twelfth Night.

Includes index.
1. Holiday cookery. 2. Entertaining. 3. Menus.
I. Title.
TX739.H33 1986   642'.4   86–7542
ISBN 0-517-56277-4

•

10   9   8   7   6   5   4   3

For
my mother and father,
Clara and John,
who first gave me the spirit of the holidays,
and
for the innocent, childlike spirit in all of us
during this happiest of seasons

•

CONTENTS

ACKNOWLEDGMENTS

*M*uch of this book is about the warm holiday spirit that we all embrace at the end of each year, and I consider myself lucky to have many people in my life who hold onto the spirit all year long, and whose support during the two years I worked on this book helped me finish it.

Over the years, I've sampled and collected recipes from my family and friends, and many of those recipes appear here. My thanks to my mother, Clara Henry; to all the Hadamuscins; and to Joe Brescia, Iva Mae Montalbano, Ron Spainhour, Evelyn Spainhour, Dana Landry, Lindsay Miller, Tom Barnes, William Barnard, Mimi Benowitz, Rose Meola, and Janet Tingey.

Many family members and friends also served as guinea pigs while I tested and retested recipes until I got them right, especially Ken Sansone, Ronni Stolzenberg, and Marty Kleinman, who cheerfully sat down to a procession of hot and heavy winter dinners on hot and heavy summer nights and who put up with me when disaster struck in the kitchen.

Others lent their possessions for photographs, just like folks borrow things in real life: Tom Barnes, Lindsay Miller, Pam Thomas, Pauline Wilkofsky, Ken Daniels, Nolan Drummond, and Mary Ann Podesta.

Thanks to everyone at Crown Publishers who was instrumental in this book becoming a reality, especially: my editor, Harriet Bell, who smoothly guided me from beginning to end while constantly offering sound advice and encouragement; Jo Fagan and Bruce Harris, who saw promise in this project right from the start; and Esther Mitgang, whose unflagging enthusiasm never dimmed. Thanks, too, to my agent, Diane Cleaver, who was always there with a helpful hand.

A special note of thanks goes to the talented young photographer Marcia Luce, who, with the able assistance of Donna Schulman, created beautiful pictures and maintained her good cheer, even when she was ready but the food wasn't. Thanks, to Rick Ellis and Nancy Kenmore, who helped to make the food picture perfect.

HAPPY HOLIDAYS

*T*his is my season! The period between Thanksgiving and Twelfth Night is my favorite time of the year. It's a season of reunion, reflection, and rebirth of spirit; a time of peace, joy, and good feelings toward all men and women; a time of unity and tolerance; a time when we act the way we should act all year long.

This is a season of tradition and celebration that seemingly changes, yet essentially remains the same. There is a calming stability in family celebrations and rituals; the preparation and celebration creates memories to last a lifetime. Traditions can be sacred or silly, but they become and remain a strong source of bonding, love, and security. The magic, mystery, decorations, presents, singing, laughter, and special foods of the holiday season are all part of the traditions lovingly handed down from generation to generation.

Christmas memories—we carry them with us all our lives. When I was growing up in Ohio, my brothers, sister, and I would leaf longingly through the "wish book" (The Sears Roebuck catalog) during the dog days of August. We would spend hours picking out hundreds of toys and other gifts we hoped to find under the tree on Christmas morning. As Christmas approached, we tried to make ourselves deserving of the best presents by putting on our best behavior and completing our chores around the farm. We would act sickeningly nicer and nicer as each day brought us closer to the big day.

I remember my mother getting the whole family into the Christmas mood. There were all the preparations, Christmas carols and candles, and all the wonderful smells that came from the kitchen. Decorations went onto the shrubs outside, the doors, windows, and just about anywhere in the house where there was a bare spot.

Now that I'm grown up and *slightly* older, the magic of the season is still with me. I've met many people of different backgrounds, faiths, and traditions who have different memories, yet many of those memories are somehow similar to my own. The world really *is* small, and we all really are not that different.

My hope is that this book will help you make new memories, enjoying the special and memorable flavors of this very special season with family and friends gathered together with down-home American goodness and simplicity, and that the joy and peace of "days gone by" will be yours again.

Happy Holidays!

"Of all the old festivals, that of Christmas awakens the strongest and most heartfelt associations."
Washington Irving

INTRODUCTION

*H*ow can we help but get into a partying spirit during the holiday season at the end of each year? A heightened sense of festivity fills the air, along with a renewed generosity of spirit. This book is intended to help make party-giving easy and enjoyable rather than dutiful drudgery. What began as a haphazard collection of recipes that I started putting together to make my own holiday entertaining easier evolved into this collection of menus covering just about every holiday entertaining need from formal Christmas dinners and an informal New Year's Day brunch to an impromptu Christmas-week supper and a tree-trimming buffet.

•

During the holiday season, many of us celebrate a heritage of food and drink having roots hundreds of years old. Also, many aspects of our celebrations have been influenced by varied ethnic backgrounds, some not even necessarily our own, that have evolved into being quintessentially American. While many new chefs and home cooks are introducing previously unknown ethnic influences and new techniques into American cuisine, many others are rediscovering the great traditions of American cooking handed down from one generation to another. Much of this renaissance is reflected in the use of native American ingredients and the renewed interest in the honest, down-home regional dishes of America, food that nourished our forebears and is just as satisfying two or three centuries later. During the holiday season, which is so bound in tradition, it seems especially appropriate to experience the joys and delights of this kind of traditional and comforting fare.

I like to make holiday entertaining as carefree as possible while still serving food steeped in tradition. Some of the recipes I've collected over the years have been handed down and some are classics that have been streamlined and updated, yet without sacrificing quality or losing that good old-fashioned flavor. In other instances, traditional holiday ingredients are used in new ways, such as the All-American Buffet Dinner or the Thanksgiving Harvest Dinner, but the familiar flavors and scents of the holiday kitchen are everpresent.

•

> "To hurry is useless. The thing to do is to set out in time."
> *Jean de la Fontaine, ca. 1650*
>
> "A place for everything, and everything in its place."
> *Isabella Mary Beeton, 1861*

The key element to successful entertaining is organization, an idea you will find stressed again and again in the pages that follow. Each menu is preceded by a section called "getting ready" to help you plot out your work schedule, including as much advance preparation and cooking as possible. To help you plan your party, suggestions for table settings and beverages, including wines, are also given with each menu, along with menu variations. The first chapter offers recipes for things to make well in advance to help you get a jump on the season, which can be stored away for your own use in entertaining or used as gifts.

With good planning, it is easy to entertain any night of the week in a relaxed manner and quite a few menus have been created especially for quick and easy entertaining, even at the end of a workday. Good planning can also save money, as well as time and steps. Make lists of both priorities and details. Check table linens, flatware, dishes, glassware, and any special serving pieces the menu may require, as well as any special cooking equipment. Remember to think of candles, fresh flowers, greens, and any other decorative elements when you shop. Always plan on having enough wine, liquor, and nonalcoholic beverages. I usually buy about half again what I will need; I never have to worry about running out, and if it isn't used up this time, it will be the next. If you've taken the bit of effort needed to plan carefully and organize your timing, you'll be in a relaxed frame of mind, and you'll enjoy the party as much as your guests do.

•

> "Always buy the freshest and best ingredients. There is absolutely no substitute for the best. Good food cannot be made of inferior ingredients."
> *James Beard, 1977*

There is an emphasis throughout this book on the fresh, seasonal ingredients available to all of us during the late fall and early winter. For example, cranberries, a favorite of mine, pop up again and again. However, fresh vegetables such as peas and asparagus never appear, because, though they may be available, they are generally too costly and almost never at their peak. (Fresh tomatoes do appear once or twice, but in preparations that make up for any out-of-season imperfections.)

Never use artificial flavorings: use pure vanilla extract, pure chocolate, and fresh sweet cream. Whenever possible use real butter (the recipes have been tested with the sweet, unsalted kind) rather than margarine.

One of my passions is black pepper, and I use very little salt.

Except where dishes cannot be easily tasted after seasoning, the recipes say "season with salt and freshly ground black pepper to taste." Do just that, and do use freshly ground pepper—the difference in flavor is immeasurable. When a recipe says "plenty of fresh pepper," it's because I think it tastes best that way, but you be the judge.

As far as herbs and spices are concerned, they can be varied to your own taste, too, but I suggest you try the recipe as written first; I think you'll find that most dishes are quite generously seasoned. Herbs specified are dried, except where noted, since many are not readily available in the late fall and winter unless you grow your own. Where fresh herbs are crucial to the recipe, they are listed in the ingredients. Use fresh herbs if you can and triple the quantity of dried herbs called for in the recipe. Where parsley is listed, it always means fresh parsley, which is always available; never use dried.

●

Every recipe in this book lists the number of servings it yields or what the end result will be, so you don't have to use Gracie Allen's mother's sure but unnecessary methods. The number of servings given is for the use of the recipe in its particular menu, so if you're using the recipe separately, don't follow that number slavishly; use your own good judgment. I always like to make sure I have enough, so you should not have to worry about skimping: if a recipe says it will serve 12 in a particular menu, it will, with seconds for some, unless you've got guests with unusually large appetites.

●

Great food and good organization are not the only key to successful entertaining. Thoughtful little touches—zany or elegant place cards, an unusual centerpiece, a grab bag—can transform a good party into a truly memorable occasion. Each menu in this book is built around a theme and suggestions are offered for table settings, food presentation ideas, background music in some cases, and other ideas that I've found help make a party special. Remember that creating a festive holiday atmosphere is really only a matter of a little extra attention to detail and an abundance of food, color, scents, music, and lights. When in doubt, overdo it!

"When my mother had to get dinner for eight, she'd just make enough for sixteen and only serve half."
Gracie Allen, 1946

"Gay nonessentials are the very essence of festivity."
Elsa Maxwell, 1954

"A lot of organization plus a bit of style matched with good food makes every guest smile."
John Hadamuscin, 1986

MAKING THINGS AHEAD

•

Lindsay Miller's Bourbon Balls

Sugarplum Pudding   Lemon Curd

Black Bourbon Fruitcake

Martha Washington's White Fruitcake

Brandied Peaches   Homemade Mincemeat

Tarragon Mustard   Hot Honey Mustard

Cranberry Liqueur   Irish Cream Liqueur

Spiced Apple Brandy Liqueur

Nut Brittle   English Toffee

Chocolate Citrus Sticks

Hard Spice Candy

Chocolate Turtles

I can't help it: right after Hallowe'en visions of sugarplums start to dance in my head. I start making lists and head for the kitchen to begin preparation for the holiday season ahead. Everything in this section can be prepared well before Thanksgiving, and many, such as the Sugarplum Pudding and fruitcakes, *should* be made well in advance so that flavors

"Forewarned, forearmed; to be prepared is half the victory."

Cervantes

can develop and ripen. Check the individual recipes early to make sure you leave yourself plenty of time.

Many of the recipes here are used later in the individual menus, giving you a head start on some of the cooking, but all of them can be given as gifts that will be happily received. Suggestions for packing each item for gift-giving are listed at the end of each recipe, following the symbol ■. Also see the photograph on page 33.

Lindsay Miller's Bourbon Balls

MAKES ABOUT 5 DOZEN

2 cups crushed vanilla wafers
1 cup confectioners' sugar
1 cup chopped walnuts *or* pecans
2 tablespoons unsweetened cocoa powder
2 tablespoons light corn syrup *or* honey
¼ to ½ cup bourbon
Confectioners' sugar

1. Mix the crushed wafers, 1 cup confectioners' sugar, nuts, cocoa, corn syrup, and bourbon together until well blended. The mixture should be moist but not soggy.

2. Roll the dough by approximate teaspoonfuls into small balls. Roll the balls in additional confectioners' sugar. Store the balls in a tightly covered tin in a cool, dry place.

■ Bourbon Balls look pretty packed in canning jars that are tied with red and green plaid ribbon bows. Or pack them in small, decorative tins that are lined with paper doilies.

My friend Lindsay is a true G.S.L.O.Q. (Grand Southern Lady Of Quality) and a great lover of Christmas. In fact, she and I first met when we lived in the same apartment building and I was decorating the lobby for the holidays. She was passing through and stopped to chat; then the next day she showed up at my door with a tin of her famous Bourbon Balls. Needless to say, we've been friends ever since!

Sugarplum Pudding

MAKES ONE 2-QUART PUDDING

This recipe differs from most plum pudding recipes in that it actually contains plums (dried prunes), along with the more usual collection of fruit. I always make this in January to be used the following holiday season (in fact I've got part of a pudding in the refrigerator right now that's almost two years old, and it tastes wonderful). The flavor can be somewhat harsh if the pudding doesn't ripen and mellow for at least six weeks. If you don't have a pudding mold, any deep, round 2-quart mold, or even coffee cans, will do, but cover them tightly with aluminum foil.

1 pound dark raisins
1 pound dried currants
1 pound dried prunes, pitted and chopped
½ cup brandy
1½ cups all-purpose flour
1 teaspoon baking powder
1 teaspoon salt
1 teaspoon ground cinnamon
½ teaspoon grated nutmeg
1 tablespoon ground ginger
¼ pound candied orange peel, chopped
¼ pound candied lemon peel, chopped
½ cup sliced almonds
1½ cups fine dry bread crumbs
½ pound beef suet, finely chopped
1¼ cups firmly packed dark brown sugar
4 large eggs, lightly beaten
1 teaspoon grated lemon rind
⅓ cup brandy *or* rum, warmed

1. Combine the raisins, currants, and prunes in a mixing bowl with the brandy and let the mixture steep for 1 hour.

2. In a very large mixing bowl, sift together the flour, baking powder, salt, and spices. Combine the fruit mixture, the orange and lemon peels, and the almonds with the flour mixture and toss until the fruits are well coated. Fold in the bread crumbs.

3. In a separate mixing bowl, combine the suet, brown sugar, eggs, and grated lemon rind. Blend this mixture into the flour-fruit mixture, making a *very* thick batter.

4. Transfer the batter to a very well greased 2-quart pudding mold and cover the mold. Stand the mold in a large stockpot or kettle, and pour hot water into the pot to come about three-quarters of the way up the side of the mold. Cover the pot and steam the pudding over medium heat for 8 hours, adding hot water as needed.

5. When the pudding is done, remove the mold from the pot and allow to cool to room temperature; then refrigerate the pudding, stored in the covered mold, for a minimum of 6 weeks.

6. To serve, allow the pudding to come to room temperature, then steam it again for 1 hour. Unmold the pudding onto a platter or heatproof, footed cakestand and garnish with a few sprigs of holly. Pour ⅓ cup warmed brandy or rum over the pudding, ignite, and serve immediately (and triumphantly!). Cut into thin slices and serve with Brandy Butter (page 124).

Note: If the pudding is to be served at a buffet, or if you just don't want to play with fire, the pudding can be glazed with ¾ cup warmed currant jelly.

Lemon Curd

MAKES 2 CUPS

1 cup fresh lemon juice (4 to 6 lemons)
¼ cup finely shredded lemon peel
1¼ cups sugar
6 tablespoons butter
3 eggs, lightly beaten

1. In a medium saucepan, combine the lemon juice, lemon peel, and sugar. Bring to a boil and simmer for 5 minutes. Add the butter and stir until it has melted. Remove the mixture from the heat and cool to room temperature.

2. Beat the eggs into the lemon-sugar mixture until well blended and place over low heat. Bring to just below the simmering point and cook, stirring constantly, for 7 to 10 minutes, or until the mixture thickens and coats the spoon.

3. Remove from heat and pour into one 2-cup or two 1-cup sterilized jars. Cool, cover, and refrigerate.

■ Pour warm lemon curd into French confiture jars or canning jars and cover. Cut 4-inch squares of green tartan or gingham plaid fabric with pinking sheers and tie them over the tops of the jars with green ribbons. Tie a few tiny jingle bells into the bows.

"The Proof is in the Pudding"

•

According to an old Yorkshire tradition, in as many homes as you eat plum pudding during the twelve days following Christmas, as many happy and lucky good months you will have during the coming year.

Another old tradition is to tuck a large coin into the pudding batter. When the pudding is served, whoever gets the slice with the coin has a whole year of good luck ahead. So, eat your pudding!

Quintessentially British and a teatime favorite, this sweet yet tart, velvety spread is heavenly on freshly baked scones, muffins, and tea breads. It also makes an excellent filling for layer cakes or baked tartlet shells. Lemon curd keeps up to two months in the refrigerator, so it can be made well ahead of time. For gift-giving double the recipe.

Black Bourbon Fruitcake

MAKES ONE 10-INCH TUBE CAKE

OR TWO 9 × 5-INCH LOAF CAKES

Here's a "southernized" version of the English classic. Don't let the long list of ingredients frighten you—this cake is an easy one to prepare. Make it well in advance so it has plenty of time to soak up plenty of bourbon. This cake will keep for a year.

¾ cup (1½ sticks) butter, softened
1¼ cups firmly packed dark brown sugar
3 large eggs
2½ cups sifted all-purpose flour
1 teaspoon baking powder
1 teaspoon salt
2 teaspoons ground cinnamon
½ teaspoon grated nutmeg
1 teaspoon ground allspice
½ cup dark molasses
½ cup brewed black coffee
½ cup bourbon
1 pound dark raisins
½ pound candied red cherries, chopped
½ pound candied green cherries, chopped
¼ pound candied orange peel, chopped
¼ pound candied lemon peel, chopped
½ pound citron, chopped
½ pound dried pitted dates, chopped
1 cup chopped pecans
Bourbon
½ cup currant jelly, warmed
Pecan halves
Candied red cherry halves

1. Preheat the oven to 300°F. Grease a 10-inch tube pan or two 9 × 5-inch loaf pans, line the bottoms with wax paper, and grease the paper.

2. In a large mixing bowl, cream together the butter and brown sugar. Beat in the eggs.

3. In a separate bowl, sift together the flour, baking powder, salt, and spices. Beat this dry mixture into the butter and sugar; then beat in the molasses, coffee, and bourbon. Fold in the fruit and nuts.

4. Carefully pack the batter into the prepared pan almost to the top. Place the pan on the center rack of the oven and bake for 2½ to 3 hours for the tube cake and 2 to 2½ hours for the loaves, or until a cake tester inserted in the center comes out clean.

5. Allow the cake to cool in the pan for 30 minutes; then remove the cake from the pan and let cool on a wire rack. Wrap carefully in a triple layer of cheesecloth which has been soaked in bourbon. Seal tightly with aluminum foil and store in a cool, dry place.

6. Once a week, remove the aluminum foil and brush additional bourbon onto the cheesecloth. The longer the cake is stored and the more times it is dowsed, the more pungent and flavorful it becomes.

7. To decorate and glaze, brush the top of the cake with the warmed currant jelly, arrange pecan halves around the perimeter and a row of cherry halves down the center, and brush again with jelly. Allow the jelly to cool before serving.

"As Nutty as a . . ."

•

Composed of fruits and nuts held together with rich batter, fruitcakes are traditional Thanksgiving and Christmas fare. The dark rich cakes are typical of Europe, from where they emigrated to America. The holiday custom goes back to the days when a cake so rich in precious fruits and nuts from distant lands was an expensive luxury that could only be afforded at special occasions. Our Colonial ancestors even competed in blending fruits and spices in new and delicious ways. Because they keep so well, these cakes are made far ahead and improve with age, especially if saturated with a little sherry, brandy, or bourbon from time to time.

Martha Washington's White Fruitcake

You can't find a more traditional cake than this one (well, I do admit to fiddling around with the recipe a bit, but Martha still gets all the credit). Legend tells us that this cake was a favorite at Mount Vernon during the holiday season. Making this cake dirties a lot of mixing bowls, but the result is well worth the bother.

1½ cups golden raisins
1 cup chopped dried apricots
½ cup brandy
½ pound candied orange peel, chopped
½ pound candied lemon peel, chopped
½ pound citron, chopped
½ pound candied pineapple, chopped
3½ cups sifted all-purpose flour
½ teaspoon salt
½ teaspoon ground mace
¼ teaspoon grated nutmeg
1½ cups (3 sticks) butter, softened
1½ cups sugar
6 large eggs, separated
¼ cup dry sherry
2 teaspoons grated lemon rind

1. The night before baking the cake, place the raisins and apricots in a medium saucepan, add the brandy, and bring to just below simmering. Remove from heat and let stand for 30 minutes; then remove the mixture to a mixing bowl and add the remaining fruit and toss well. Cover well and allow to stand overnight.

2. Preheat the oven to 325°F. Grease a 10-inch tube pan or two 9 × 5-inch loaf pans.

3. Stir the flour, salt, and spices together in a mixing bowl until well blended. In a separate large mixing bowl, cream together the butter and half of the sugar.

4. In another small bowl, beat the egg yolks until they begin to thicken; then beat them into the butter and sugar. Slowly beat in the remaining sugar and then the flour mixture. Next beat in the sherry and then stir in the fruit mixture and grated lemon rind.

5. In a separate bowl, beat the egg whites until stiff. Fold them into the batter; then immediately pour the batter into the prepared cake pan.

6. Place a shallow pan of hot water on the bottom rack of the oven; then place the cake pan on the center rack. Bake about 1¼ hours for loaf cakes, 1¾ hours for the tube cake, or until a cake tester inserted in the cake comes out clean.

7. Let the cake cool in the pan for 20 minutes; then remove the cake from the pan and let cool on a wire rack. Wrap in a triple layer of cheesecloth which has been soaked in sherry; then wrap tightly in aluminum foil and store in a cool, dry place. Weekly, remove the aluminum foil and brush on more sherry; then rewrap tightly.

■ Wrap the fruitcakes in clean aluminum foil and tie with wide silver ribbons. Tuck a card under the ribbon explaining the soaking process. *Or* remove the foil and cheesecloth and wrap the fruit-cakes well with plastic wrap and tie them with wide shiny red or green ribbons.

Brandied Peaches

Ripe, firm peaches, peeled, pitted, and halved
Whole cloves
Sugar
Brandy
Cinnamon sticks

1. Stud each peach half with 3 cloves. Fill sterilized 1-quart canning jars with the peaches, without crowding.

2. Mix equal amounts of sugar and brandy in a covered jar. Shake to mix and quickly pour over the peaches to cover. Gently push a cinnamon stick into each jar, and seal.

3. Every few days gently turn the jars upside down until the sugar has dissolved, then turn the jars upright to store.

■ Cover the lids of the canning jars with round crocheted or paper doilies and tie them on with green velvet ribbons.

These should stand at least four weeks to allow the peaches to get good and drunk! Or better yet, make these during the summer when peaches are plentiful.

Homemade Mincemeat

Homemade mincemeat in beribboned jars makes a thoughtful and practical present, so if you want enough for gift-giving, double the recipe. The list of ingredients is long, but the mincemeat is quite easy to make. The food processor is a big help in chopping the beef, suet, orange, and lemon, but dice the apples by hand for a better texture. Mincemeat should be made at least two weeks before using to allow the flavors to mellow.

1 pound lean beef, finely chopped (not ground)
1 pound beef suet, finely chopped
1 cup dark molasses
1½ pounds dark brown sugar
3 cups apple cider, preferably fresh
2 pounds dark raisins
1½ pounds dried currants
¼ pound citron, finely chopped
1 orange with peel, seeded and finely chopped
1 lemon with peel, seeded and finely chopped
1 cup brandy *or* rum
1½ teaspoons ground cinnamon
1 teaspoon ground mace
1½ teaspoons ground cloves
½ teaspoon grated nutmeg
1 teaspoon salt
½ teaspoon freshly ground black pepper
2 pounds tart apples, peeled and diced
Brandy *or* rum

1. In a large heavy saucepan, combine all of the ingredients except the apples and the final brandy or rum and bring the mixture to a simmer over low heat. Simmer, uncovered, for 1 hour, stirring occasionally. Add the apples and continue simmering until the apples are tender but not mushy, about 15 minutes.

2. Ladle the mincemeat into sterilized jars and pour enough brandy or rum over each one to cover; then seal and store in a cool, dark place. (Plastic containers can also be used, but the mincemeat should then be refrigerated.) Stir the mincemeat well before using.

■ Cover the lids of the jars with round crocheted doilies tied on with red calico ribbons. Tie a sprig of velvet holly into the bows.

Warm Mincemeat Sundaes This is a simple idea borrowed from Julia Child's inspiring Julia Child & Company series. Simply combine about ¼ cup Homemade Mincemeat and 1 tablespoon brandy or rum per person in a small heavy saucepan. Warm over low heat; then spoon over goblets of vanilla, maple-walnut, or rum-raisin ice cream.

Tarragon Mustard

MAKES 2 CUPS

*T*his mustard is similar to a Dijon-style prepared mustard, but with the subtle flavor of tarragon added. Use it on vegetables, in salad dressings, and stirred into mayonnaise.

½ cup dry mustard
¼ cup boiling water
½ cup dry white wine
½ cup white wine vinegar
1 tablespoon all-purpose flour
1 teaspoon sugar
3 tablespoons chopped fresh tarragon *or* 4 teaspoons dried tarragon
¼ teaspoon ground allspice
1 teaspoon salt

1. Combine the mustard and water in a small bowl and let the mixture stand for 1 hour.

2. In a small heavy saucepan, combine the mustard mixture with the remaining ingredients and bring to a simmer over medium heat, stirring constantly. Lower heat and simmer, stirring constantly, until the mixture has thickened, about 3 to 5 minutes.

3. Remove from heat, transfer the mustard to a small mixing bowl, and allow to cool. Cover tightly with aluminum foil or plastic wrap, and refrigerate overnight.

4. Remove the mustard from the refrigerator, and beat the mixture with a fork or whisk until very smooth. Place the mustard in jars, and store, tightly covered, in the refrigerator.

Hot Honey Mustard

MAKES ABOUT 2 CUPS

This fiery sweet-and-sour mustard holds its own with strong-flavored meats, from country ham to kielbasa. A small amount is good when blended into sautéed or stir-fried vegetables, too. If you can get dry mustard in bulk, double or triple the recipe and give small jars as gifts. Put a note on the label that it should be refrigerated, and that it's hot, hot, hot.

¾ cup dry mustard
¾ cup white vinegar
⅔ cup honey
2 large egg yolks

1. Combine the mustard and vinegar in a small bowl and stir to blend. Cover and let stand overnight at room temperature.

2. In a small heavy saucepan, combine the mustard-vinegar mixture and the honey and egg yolks. Place over low heat and cook, stirring constantly, until thickened. Cover and store in the refrigerator.

■ Small earthenware crocks or confiture jars, available in kitchenware shops, make charming gift containers for mustards.

Cranberry Liqueur

MAKES ABOUT 1 QUART

This ruby-red liqueur, served in a faceted crystal decanter, makes a wonderful ending to any dinner party. Make it at least five weeks before you want to use it.

2 cups sugar
1 cup water
3 cups (1 12-ounce package) cranberries, coarsely chopped
1 teaspoon grated orange rind
3 cups vodka

1. Combine the sugar and water in a medium saucepan over low heat and bring to a boil. Lower the heat and simmer, stirring constantly, until all of the sugar has dissolved. Stir in the cranberries and orange rind and remove from heat. Cool to room temperature.

2. In a large glass container, combine the syrup-cranberry mixture with the vodka and cover tightly. Store 3 to 4 weeks in a cool, dark place, shaking the container or stirring every 2 or 3 days.

3. Place a sieve over a bowl and drain the berries, reserving the liquid. Press the berries against the sieve to extract as much liquid as possible. Discard the berries.

4. Strain the liquid through a double thickness of cheesecloth and repeat the process until the liquid is clear. Pour the liquid into a 1-quart bottle or decanter or two 1-pint bottles, cover tightly and store in a cool, dark place for two weeks before using.

Spiced Berry Brandy Substitute 5 cups of brandy for the vodka and lemon rind for the orange rind. Add 1 teaspoon *each* of whole cloves and whole allspice and a cinnamon stick to the sugar syrup in step 1 before adding the berries. Makes 1½ quarts (3 pints).

■ Pretty and inexpensive glass bottles are available at kitchenware shops, or save fancy clear bottles from store-bought liqueurs. Tie a green velvet ribbon around the collar of each bottle and tuck a sprig of holly into the bow. Cranberry liqueur makes a spectacular gift with a set of cordial glasses or inside a crystal decanter.

Irish Cream Liqueur

MAKES ABOUT 3 QUARTS

*S*ipping a glass of this liqueur while relaxing in front of a cozy fire is one of the true delights of a cold winter evening. Warning: this smooth and creamy liqueur may go down like a glass of cool chocolate milk, but oh, what a kick!

Spice Bags

•

Here is a quick and simple gift when you need one on the spur of the moment: Make small packets containing 3 cinnamon sticks, 2 teaspoons whole allspice, and 2 teaspoons whole cloves by tying them up in 6-inch squares of cheesecloth with kitchen string, then pack the packets in small jars or tins or small plastic bags to keep the spices fresh. Tie it all up with ribbons and include instructions for making mulled cider or wine (see pages 72 and 66). You might even give a jug of wine or cider, too.

4 cups Irish whiskey
2 14-ounce cans sweetened condensed milk
1 ounce semisweet chocolate, melted and cooled
¾ teaspoon almond extract
2 teaspoons vanilla extract
6 large eggs
2 cups light cream *or* half-and-half

1. Combine all of the ingredients in a blender or food processor and blend until smooth.

2. Store in tightly covered bottles or jars in the refrigerator at least 2 weeks before using. Keeps up to 6 weeks.

■ Pour the mixture into old whiskey bottles after soaking off the labels. Wrap the bottles in aluminum foil and tie lacy ribbons around the collars. Don't forget to put a note on the gift card telling the recipient to refrigerate the liqueur and how long it will keep.

Spiced Apple Brandy Liqueur

MAKES 2 QUARTS

This not only makes a wonderful after-dinner drink, but has an added bonus: the leftover strained apples are delicious served over ice cream or gingerbread.

8 medium tart apples, cored and quartered
4 cinnamon sticks
2 teaspoons whole cloves
2 teaspoons whole allspice
4 cups dry white jug wine
4 cups sugar
4 cups brandy
½ teaspoon grated lemon rind

1. In a medium saucepan, combine the apples, spices, and ½ cup white wine. Place over medium heat and bring to a simmer. Cook, loosely covered, for about 7 minutes, or until the apples begin to soften. Stir in the sugar and cook, stirring until the sugar has dissolved.

2. Combine the apple mixture, the remaining wine, and the brandy in a large glass container. Cover tightly and store in a cool, dark place, shaking the container every 2 or 3 days, for 3 weeks.

3. Strain the liquid through a double thickness of cheesecloth and repeat until the liquid is clear. Reserve the "drunken" apples for another use. Pour the liqueur into two 1-quart or four 1-pint decanters or bottles, cover tightly, and store in a cool, dark place for 1 or 2 weeks before using.

■ Use pretty bottles or decanters, available at kitchenware shops, and tie a red velvet ribbon around the collar of each bottle. Tie a few silvery jingle bells into each bow.

Nut Brittle

*E*ver since I was a kid, nut brittle has been one of my favorite candies. Try different kinds of nuts—peanuts are just fine, but I like using pecans, cashews, or Brazil nuts—or a combina-tion. Nut brittle keeps well, so it's great for gift-giving.

1 cup light corn syrup
2¼ cups sugar
1 cup water
2 cups chopped unsalted nuts
¾ teaspoon salt
2 tablespoons butter
½ teaspoon baking soda
2 teaspoons vanilla extract

1. In a heavy saucepan, combine the corn syrup, sugar, and water and stir to blend. Place over medium-high heat and bring to a boil. Stir until the sugar has dissolved; then continue cooking, without stirring, until the mixture reaches 250°F. on a candy thermometer.

2. Stir in the nuts and continue cooking until the mixture reaches 300°F., stirring occasionally. Remove from heat and quickly, yet thoroughly, stir in the butter, baking soda, salt, and vanilla.

3. Working quickly, pour the mixture onto a greased baking sheet and spread into as thin a layer as possible. As the candy begins to cool, turn it over with your hands and stretch it out even more until it very thin and translucent.

4. Allow the candy to cool completely; then break it up into rough, bite-size pieces. Store in tightly covered containers lined with wax paper.

■ Pack nut brittle into glass jars and tie thick red yarn around the collars, or pack it into small decorative tins.

English Toffee

The recipe for this authentic and mouth-watering toffee comes from Janet Tingey, whose family has passed it down for generations. This recipe makes plenty of candy for storing and giving. For a quick and scrumptious dessert, try sprinkling some coarsely chopped toffee over big scoops of vanilla or chocolate ice cream.

½ pound walnuts *or* almonds, ground
1 pound milk chocolate, grated
2½ cups sugar
2 cups (4 sticks) butter
4 tablespoons light corn syrup
⅓ pound walnuts *or* almonds, finely chopped
1 cup water

1. Spread half of the ground nuts in a thin, even layer over the bottom of an ungreased baking sheet or two 9-inch cake pans; then spread half of the chocolate in an even layer over the nuts.

2. Combine the sugar, butter, corn syrup, chopped nuts, and water in a heavy saucepan and place over medium heat. Cook, stirring constantly with a heavy wooden spoon, until a candy thermometer reads 280°F. Remove from heat and allow thermometer temperature to reach 285°F.; then immediately pour the syrup over the nut and chocolate layers. Let cool for 10 minutes.

3. Sprinkle the remaining grated chocolate evenly over the cooling syrup; then sprinkle on the remaining ground nuts. Let stand for at least 5 hours; then break into bite-size pieces. Store in tightly covered containers.

■ Pack the toffee in doily-lined glass jars and tie a green velvet ribbon around the collars of the jars, or pack in decorative tins.

Chocolate Citrus Sticks

MAKES ABOUT 5 DOZEN

What a perfect accompaniment to after-dinner coffee or tea these make: they're refreshing, satisfying, and hard to resist even at the end of a big meal. These keep indefinitely, so you may want to double the recipe. Use grapefruit, orange, lemon, or tangerine rinds, or a combination.

4 oranges *or* 3 grapefruit *or* 6 lemons *or* tangerines
2½ cups sugar
2½ cups water
6 ounces semisweet chocolate

1. Cut the fruit in half and remove the flesh (reserve for another use), saving only the colored zest and white pith of the fruit rind. Cut the rind into strips about ¼ inch wide and 2 to 3 inches long.

2. Drop the strips into a pan of cold water, place over medium-high heat, and bring to a boil. Drain and repeat the process three more times. During the last boiling, continue cooking and simmer for 30 minutes. Drain again and reserve the strips.

3. Combine the sugar with 2½ cups water in the saucepan over medium heat and stir to dissolve the sugar. Add the rind strips to the pan and bring to a boil. Lower the heat and simmer for 10 to 15 minutes, or until the fruit strips become translucent and tender.

4. Remove the fruit strips from the pan with a slotted spoon and place them onto a wire rack. Allow them to dry for 8 hours or overnight.

5. Melt the chocolate in the top of a double boiler over simmering water. With small tongs or using two forks, dip the fruit strips into the chocolate a few at a time to coat. Remove to a sheet of aluminum foil and allow the chocolate to set. Store in a tightly covered container in the refrigerator.

Sugared Citrus Sticks Instead of coating with the chocolate, roll the strips in granulated sugar while they are still warm; then allow to dry for 8 hours or overnight.

Hard Spice Candy

3 cups sugar
1 cup light corn syrup
Food coloring (see below)
1 cup water
¼ teaspoon flavoring (see below)
Confectioners' sugar

Pounds and pounds of these candies are made and sold every Christmas by the women of the First United Methodist Church in my hometown of Willard, Ohio. They've long been a favorite of mine, and my mother sends me a care package of them every December. Make several batches, using the different flavoring/coloring suggestions below.

Flavoring	*Food Coloring*
Oil of spearmint	3 drops yellow and 4 drops blue
Oil of peppermint	6 drops blue
Oil of cinnamon	7 drops red
Oil of orange or tangerine	4 drops yellow and 3 drops red
Oil of root beer	3 drops red, 2 drops blue, and 2 drops yellow
Oil of clove	3 drops blue and 3 drops red
Oil of pineapple	4 drops yellow

1. Mix together the sugar, syrup, food coloring, and water. Bring to a boil and continue boiling until the temperature reaches 305°F. on a candy thermometer (hard-crack stage—threads of syrup dripped into cold water should become hard and brittle). Remove from heat, allow to cool to about 250°F., and stir in the flavoring oil.

2. Pour the hot syrup onto a cool greased baking sheet (or a marble slab) in a thin layer and allow to cool.

3. Break the candy into bite-size pieces and dust them lightly with confectioners' sugar. Store in jars or tins.

■ A variety of these candies in a rainbow of colors looks nice packed in fancy clear glass jars. Cushion the bottom of the jar with a bit of white tissue paper before packing. Tie the collars of the jars with red or white satin ribbon with a few tiny jingle bells tied into each bow.

Chocolate Turtles

MAKES 50 TURTLES

When I was a kid, our neighbor Alice Williams always made turtles at Christmastime and brought over a big tin of them. To this day, they're one of my favorite holiday treats.

150 pecan halves (about 3 cups)
50 caramels
8 ounces semisweet chocolate

1. Preheat the oven to 300°F.

2. On greased baking sheets, arrange the pecan halves in groups of three (end to end) flat side down. Place a caramel on top of each cluster.

3. Place in the oven until the caramels soften, about 5 to 8 minutes. Remove from the oven and flatten the caramels over the pecans with a buttered spoon. Cool slightly.

4. Melt the chocolate in the top of a double boiler over simmering water. Dip the turtles into the chocolate and cool on wax paper. Store in tightly covered containers in a cool place.

■ Pack chocolate turtles in decorative tins. Tie a toy turtle on top with a ribbon.

MAKING THINGS AHEAD offers a pretty and mouth-watering array of extraspecial gifts from the kitchen (clockwise from bottom): glazed and unglazed Black Bourbon Fruitcakes; Sugarplum Pudding in its mold; Bourbon Balls; Nut Brittle; Spiced Apple Brandy and Homemade Cranberry liqueurs; Homemade Mincemeat in doily-topped, beribboned jars; Brandied Peaches; and Lemon Curd and Tarragon Mustard in fabric-topped jars.

A WASSAILING BUFFET SUPPER for the week before Christmas welcomes chilled carolers with a roaring fire after they make their rounds (clockwise from center): a spice-scented Mulled Cider Wassail Bowl; Country Thyme Pâté and Spinach Pesto Pâté; an assortment of breads, sausages, and homemade mustards; Onion-Rosemary Tartlets on an antique cabbage shredder; machine-popped popcorn served in an antique popper; and a basket of homemade cookies, including Grandma Stapleton's Bohemian Butter Cookies, Date and Almond Pinwheels, Betty Lou's Pecan Toffee Bars, and Butternut Balls.

A HARVEST DINNER

•

FOR 8 TO 10

MENU

Cheddar Cheese Straws

Cream of Mushroom and Onion Soup

Roasted Turkey with Pan Juices

Cranberry–Pecan Stuffing

*Steamed Brussels Sprouts and Baby Carrots
with Two Mustards*

Glazed Yams and Granny Smith Apples

Oven-Braised Leeks

Jalapeño–Cornmeal Biscuits

Pumpkin–Mincemeat Tart with Ginger Cream

Homemade Cranberry Liqueur (page 25)

I used to think Thanksgiving dinner—turkey and the usual array of trimmings—was a rather heavy and humdrum affair. Over the last few years, I've played with the traditional elements until this streamlined menu evolved. This "new traditional" dinner makes preparation easier for the cook and digestion easier on the diners. None of the essential flavors have been omitted, but in some cases they have been combined.

Thanksgiving wouldn't be Thanksgiving without a turkey, but

"Over the river and through the wood,
Now grandmother's cap I spy!
Hurrah for the fun!
Is the pudding done?
Hurrah for the pumpkin pie!"
Lydia Maria Child

AN ANYTIME SUPPER on Christmas Eve can be relaxed and relaxing; everything here can be made in advance and then served up in the kitchen at a few moments notice (clockwise from bottom): Burlington Brown Bread; Ken's Fish and Corn Chowder served from the stockpot; Cranberry-Nut Pudding; and Christmas Ribbon Slaw.

with a Cranberry–Pecan Stuffing the need for both stuffing and a sweet cranberry sauce is eliminated. Apples appear with yams rather than in the traditional pie, and glazed leeks are a simple and pretty replacement for rich creamed onions. Finally, the Pumpkin–Mincemeat Tart puts two favorites together in a far more interesting way than in the two traditional pies. The Jalapeño–Cornmeal Biscuits add a piquant touch to this otherwise Yankee-inspired dinner. The only thing missing here is mashed potatoes, which somehow seem redundant in a meal already containing both stuffing and yams, but if you want to be a purist and serve them, along with the requisite gravy, by all means go right ahead.

Getting Ready: This is a big menu, but it requires very little last-minute preparation. The Cream of Mushroom and Onion Soup and the Pumpkin–Mincemeat Tart can be made a day ahead, and the Cranberry Liqueur should be made well in advance (page 25). The Cheddar Cheese Straws can also be made two or three weeks in advance and kept in a tightly covered container.

The Cranberry–Pecan Stuffing can be made early on Thanksgiving morning, but do not stuff the turkey until just before it goes into the oven, since bacteria can materialize. The roasting time of the turkey depends on the size—check the recipe and plan accordingly.

The leeks can be cleaned and pared and the yams parboiled a day ahead or in the morning, but do not assemble either until just before putting them into the oven, about an hour before serving.

About half an hour before serving, put the soup on the stove over very low heat and warm it up very slowly (do not boil). The Brussels sprouts and carrots, which can also be cleaned and pared early in the day, should be put on to steam about 15 minutes before serving the main course.

Mix the dough for the biscuits just before taking the turkey out of the oven. After taking the bird out of the oven to rest before being carved, turn up the oven to 425°F., and then shape the biscuits and pop them into the oven.

The ginger cream for the tart is best when whipped just before serving. It only takes a few minutes, but it can be whipped early in the day and then refrigerated.

Beverages: Thanksgiving is a purely American holiday, and the wines should be American ones. Before dinner, serve a California dry sherry, or make Cranberry Mimosas (page 96) or nonalcoholic spritzers by adding a splash of club soda to a stemmed glass of chilled, sweetened cranberry juice. A nice accompaniment to the main course would be a chilled Gamay Beaujolais or Gamay Noir. With dessert, serve a sweet Sauternes or a Riesling from California.

As a grand finale, you can proudly serve your Homemade Cranberry Liqueur.

Setting: An overflowing cornucopia is the traditional Thanksgiving symbol of harvest and abundance, but I prefer to fill a low vine basket with small pumpkins, bright gourds and squashes and then arrange some bittersweet twigs with their bright orange-red berries among them, along with some autumn leaves. Use a natural-colored, homespun tablecloth, or keep the table bare, and use heavy brass candlesticks with off-white candles.

Menu Variations: Try the Corn Bread Pudding (page 114) as an alternate stuffing for the turkey, and serve the Cranberry–Pear Tart (page 153) for dessert. As an alternate to the Steamed Brussels Sprouts and Carrots with Two Mustards, try the Julienne of Carrots and Zucchini on page 220, but double the recipe.

This dinner is an excellent one for Christmas Day, too, for those who want a Christmas turkey. Add one of the fruitcakes (pages 18–21) or the Sugarplum Pudding (page 16) for dessert.

Cheddar Cheese Straws

MAKES ABOUT 6 DOZEN

An American classic, and a quick and easy substitute for cheese and crackers at cocktail time, these will keep several weeks stored in a tightly covered container.

1 pound sharp Cheddar cheese, grated
½ cup (1 stick) butter, softened
½ teaspoon paprika
¼ teaspoon cayenne pepper
½ teaspoon salt
3 cups sifted all-purpose flour

1. Preheat the oven to 400°F.

2. Using an electric mixer, cream the cheese and butter together; then add the remaining ingredients and mix until well blended.

3. On a floured board, roll the dough into a rectangle ¼ inch thick. Cut the dough into strips approximately ½ inch × 4 inches. Holding each strip between your thumbs and forefingers, twist the strips several times and placed them 1 inch apart onto ungreased baking sheets.

4. Bake until golden brown, about 5 to 7 minutes. Remove to wire racks to cool.

Caraway Cheese Straws Add 1 teaspoon caraway seeds to the dough at the end of step 2.

39

Cream of Mushroom and Onion Soup

SERVES 8 TO 10

½ cup (1 stick) butter
6 large red onions, roughly sliced
1 pound mushrooms, coarsely chopped
6 cups hot chicken stock
2 tablespoons butter
2 tablespoons all-purpose flour
¾ cup brandy
3 cups heavy cream
Salt and freshly ground black pepper
Snipped chives

1. Divide the ½ cup butter evenly between a large heavy saucepan or Dutch oven and a large heavy skillet. Add the onions to the Dutch oven and the mushrooms to the skillet.

2. Sauté the onions over medium-high heat until they are very soft and golden brown, about 20 to 30 minutes. Meanwhile, sauté the mushrooms over medium-high heat until they are dark brown and have lost most of their moisture. Stir the contents of both pans regularly to prevent sticking.

3. Remove all the onions and half of the mushrooms to the bowl of a food processor fitted with a metal chopping blade. Reserve the remaining mushrooms. Add 1 cup chicken stock to the processor bowl and process until smoothly pureed.

4. Melt the 2 tablespoons butter in the empty large saucepan or Dutch oven. Stir in the flour to form a smooth paste. Gradually stir in 1 cup stock; then slowly add the remaining stock, stirring constantly to maintain smoothness. Stir in the brandy and mushroom-onion puree and simmer for 10 minutes.

5. Stir in the reserved sautéed mushrooms and cream and bring the soup *just* to the simmering point. *Do not boil.* Season with salt and plenty of freshly ground black pepper.

6. Serve in warmed soup bowls garnished with snipped chives and an extra grinding of black pepper.

"Strange to see how a good dinner and feasting reconciles everybody."
Samuel Pepys

Roasted Turkey with Pan Juices

SERVES 8 TO 10 WITH PLENTY OF LEFTOVERS

Thanksgiving dinner would not be complete without "the bird." The best value in turkey is a fresh or nonbasting frozen one. Self-basting ones are filled with additives and coconut or palm oil. Also, frozen turkeys with "butter" in their names may not contain any butter at all. Read the label carefully.

I always roast a larger turkey than necessary because sandwiches made from leftover turkey are one of my favorite things about Thanksgiving, and I'm partial to turkey croquettes (recipe on page 48). If you prefer to minimize the leftovers, a 12- to 15-pound turkey should be plenty for 8 to 10 people.

1 18- to 20-pound turkey
Salt and freshly ground black pepper
Cranberry–Pecan Stuffing (recipe follows)
¼ cup (½ stick) butter, softened
Dry red wine (optional)
Parsley

1. Preheat the oven to 325°F. Rinse the turkey well, inside and out, and pat dry with paper towels. Rub salt and pepper into both the neck and body cavities.

2. Stuff both cavities loosely with stuffing and close both ends with trussing skewers and string. Place the turkey breast up on a rack in a large roasting pan. Rub the skin lightly with softened butter. Insert a meat thermometer into the thickest part of the thigh without touching the bone.

3. Place the turkey in the oven and roast about 12 minutes per pound (15 minutes per pound if the turkey weighs less than 15 pounds), basting every 30 minutes with the pan juices. The turkey is done when the meat thermometer registers 180°F., or when the juices run clear when the thigh is pricked with a fork.

4. Remove the turkey to a warm platter and cover loosely with aluminum foil. Let it rest for 20 to 30 minutes before carving.

5. Scrape all particles from the bottom of the roasting pan and stir them into the pan juices to give them a deeper color and a heartier flavor. Add a small amount of water or dry red wine and salt and pepper to taste; then simmer for a few minutes on top of the stove. Remove to a warmed gravy boat.

6. Remove the stuffing to a warmed vegetable bowl. Serve the turkey surrounded with parsley. As each serving is carved, spoon a tablespoonful or so of the pan juices over each one.

Cranberry-Pecan Stuffing

MAKES ABOUT 8 CUPS

6 cups whole wheat bread cubes
½ cup sugar
½ cup water
2 cups fresh cranberries
1 cup chopped onion
1 cup diced celery
1 cup (2 sticks) butter
½ cup orange juice
1 teaspoon grated orange rind
1 cup chopped pecans
½ teaspoon ground allspice
Salt and freshly ground black pepper
2 large eggs, lightly beaten

1. Spread the bread cubes in an even layer on a baking sheet and toast in a 300°F. oven until well browned, about 10 to 15 minutes. Remove from the oven and set aside.

2. While the bread is toasting, put the sugar and water into a medium saucepan and bring to a boil, stirring to dissolve the sugar. Boil about 5 minutes, until it becomes syrupy.

3. Add the cranberries to the saucepan and let them simmer until the first few berries begin to pop, about 5 minutes. Remove from heat immediately and let the berries sit in the syrup for 5 minutes. Remove the cranberries to a large mixing bowl with a slotted spoon, draining off the syrup.

4. Sauté the onion and celery in the butter until crisp-tender, about 7 to 10 minutes. Add to the mixing bowl.

5. Add the toasted bread cubes and the remaining ingredients to the mixing bowl and toss lightly to combine. Taste and correct the seasoning with salt and pepper.

Steamed Brussels Sprouts and Baby Carrots with Two Mustards

SERVES 8 TO 10

1½ pounds Brussels sprouts
1½ pounds baby carrots
¼ cup (½ stick) butter
2 tablespoons grainy mustard
1 tablespoon Dijon mustard
Salt and freshly ground black pepper
2 tablespoons chopped parsley

1. Trim the ends of the Brussels sprouts and score an X into each end to ensure even cooking. Remove any tough outer leaves and wash carefully under cold running water to remove any sandy particles.

2. Peel the carrots (if using large carrots, cut into half lengthwise; then cut halves into 1½-inch lengths). Place the carrots in a vegetable steamer and steam over medium heat for 10 to 15 minutes, or until they're just beginning to become tender.

3. Add the Brussels sprouts to the steamer and steam the vegetables for an additional 7 to 10 minutes, or until the sprouts are crisp-tender and a vivid green.

4. Carefully remove the steamer basket of vegetables from the pan and pour off the steaming water. Add the butter, mustards, and salt and pepper to taste to the pan and stir until the butter has melted. Add the vegetables and cover tightly. Lift up the pan and shake vigorously, holding the cover on, to combine the vegetables and coat them evenly with the butter and mustards.

5. Remove to a vegetable dish and garnish with chopped parsley.

"I wish the bald eagle had not been chosen as the representative of our country; he is a bird of bad moral character. The turkey is a much more noble and respectable bird, and withal a true original native of America."
Benjamin Franklin

Glazed Yams and Granny Smith Apples

SERVES 8 TO 10

3 pounds yams
4 cups thinly sliced Granny Smith apples
¼ cup (½ stick) butter
4 tablespoons dark brown sugar
Ground cinnamon
Grated nutmeg
Salt and freshly ground black pepper

1. Place the unpeeled yams in a medium saucepan with water to cover and boil until almost tender, about 20 minutes. Peel and cut the yams into ¼-inch-thick slices.

2. Preheat the oven to 325°F. Butter a flat 2-quart baking dish. Layer the bottom of the baking dish with half of the yams, followed by half of the apples. Dot with 2 tablespoons butter, then sprinkle with 2 tablespoons brown sugar and seasonings to taste. Repeat.

3. Cover and bake for 30 minutes. Remove the cover and continue baking for an additional 25 to 30 minutes, or until the apples are soft and the surface is browned and glazed. Serve hot.

Oven-Braised Leeks

SERVES 8 TO 10

20 medium leeks
¼ cup (½ stick) butter, softened
1½ cups chicken stock

1. Preheat the oven to 325°F.

2. Trim the root ends of the leeks, and remove any tough outer leaves. Trim the leeks to a fairly uniform length, about 7 to 8 inches. Wash the leeks carefully under cold running water to remove any sandy particles between the leaves.

"Where is the man that can live without dining?"
Owen Meredith

44

3. Place the leeks in a flat baking dish in two flat layers. Smear the surface of the leeks with butter and add the stock. Bake, loosely covered with a lid or aluminum foil, until almost all the liquid has evaporated and the leeks are tender and golden, about 30 minutes.

Jalapeño-Cornmeal Biscuits

MAKES ABOUT 20

Southeast meets Southwest in these zesty biscuits. Try them as an hors d'oeuvre, split and layered with slivers of country ham and Hot Honey Mustard (page 24).

¾ cup milk
¾ cup yellow cornmeal
2 tablespoons shortening
2 jalapeño peppers, finely chopped
1 cup sifted all-purpose flour
½ teaspoon salt
4 teaspoons baking powder

1. Preheat the oven to 425°F. Scald the milk in a small heavy saucepan over medium heat.

2. While the milk is heating, combine the cornmeal and shortening in a mixing bowl. Gradually stir in the scalded milk until the shortening has melted and the mixture is smooth; then stir in the chopped jalapeño. Allow to cool to room temperature.

3. Sift the flour, salt, and baking powder together and stir into the cornmeal-milk mixture until just combined. Do not overmix.

4. Remove the dough to a well-floured board and press out to a ½-inch-thick layer with well-floured hands. Cut with a small floured biscuit cutter and place on an ungreased baking sheet.

5. Bake for 12 to 15 minutes, or until the biscuits are golden brown. Serve hot with sweet butter and honey.

Pumpkin-Mincemeat Tart

MAKES ONE 10-INCH TART

*T*his tasty tart is the perfect marriage of textures and flavors, smooth creamy pumpkin custard layered onto fruit-laden, spicy mincemeat. It's quite rich, so serve it in thin slices, but do serve it with a dollop of Ginger Cream.

1 recipe Pastry Crust (page 47)
1 cup Homemade Mincemeat (page 22)
½ cup chopped walnuts
2 cups pumpkin puree (fresh or canned)
3 eggs, lightly beaten
1⅔ cups half-and-half
½ cup firmly packed light brown sugar
¼ cup pure maple syrup
1 teaspoon ground cinnamon
½ teaspoon grated nutmeg
½ teaspoon ground ginger
½ teaspoon ground cloves
11 walnut halves

1. Preheat the oven to 400°F. Roll out the pastry crust to fit a 10-inch tart tin with removable bottom (or a 10-inch pie pan) and place in the pan, carefully pressing the dough against the fluted edges.

2. Spread the mincemeat evenly over the bottom of the pastry shell. Spread the chopped walnuts over the mincemeat.

3. In a large mixing bowl, combine the remaining ingredients except the walnut halves. Beat until smooth. Pour over the mincemeat and walnuts in the tart tin.

4. Bake for 15 minutes; then lower the oven temperature to 350°. Bake for an additional 50 to 60 minutes, or until a knife inserted in the center of the tart comes out clean. Remove to a wire rack and cool to room temperature. The tart can be refrigerated at this point, loosely covered with aluminum foil, but is best brought back to room temperature before serving.

5. Remove the outer rim of the tart tin just before serving and place the tart on a flat serving dish decorated with a paper doily. To garnish, place 1 walnut half in the center of the tart; then arrange the remaining halves around the rim of the tart, evenly spaced. Serve each thin slice with a dollop of Ginger Cream (page 210).

Pastry Crust

MAKES CRUST FOR ONE 10-INCH PIE OR TART

Use this basic crust recipe for desserts—for a savory crust, omit the sugar.

2 cups all-purpose flour
½ teaspoon salt
2 teaspoons sugar
⅓ cup vegetable shortening, chilled
⅓ cup cold butter
4 to 6 tablespoons cold water

1. Sift the flour, salt, and sugar together in a large mixing bowl; then add the shortening and butter. Using your fingertips, rub the dry ingredients and fats together until coarse and crumbly in texture. Do this quickly to keep the fats cold and solid, and do not overwork. *Or* use a pastry blender to combine the dry ingredients and shortenings.

2. Starting with 4 tablespoons, add the water and work into the flour-shortening mixture to form a ball of dough. Add 1 or 2 more tablespoons of water if necessary to hold the dough together. Wrap the dough ball in plastic wrap and chill for 1 hour before using.

3. Roll the chilled dough ball out on a floured pastry board or marble pastry slab into a circle approximately 13 inches in diameter and ⅛ inch thick. For tartlets, divide the dough and roll out each piece separately.

4. To line the pan, fold the dough into quarters and center the point in the bottom of the pan. Gently unfold the circle and press the dough into the pan. For pies, trim off the edges and crimp with your fingers. For tarts, simply trim off the excess dough.

5. Prick the surface of the dough all over with a fork. For recipes requiring prebaked shells, weight the bottom with pie weights or dry beans and bake in a preheated 450°F. oven for 10 to 15 minutes, or until lightly browned. Otherwise, cover and refrigerate or freeze until needed.

Note: To bake an unfilled pie or tart shell, first preheat the oven to 450°F. Weight the surface of the unbaked crust with dried beans and bake for about 12 minutes or until the crust is golden brown. Remove the beans and allow the crust to cool to room temperature before filling.

Leftover Pastry "Cookies"

•

Whenever my mother made pies or apple dumplings we always looked forward to having these "cookies" more than the pie!

Roll out the leftover pastry scraps into a rectangle and dot with butter. Add a sprinkling of brown sugar and a pinch of cinnamon. Roll it all up lengthwise, and place on a small piece of aluminum foil, then bake with the pie or tart until browned, about 15 minutes. Slice it into cookies when it comes out of the oven.

Turkey Croquettes

MAKES 10 CROQUETTES

Croquettes have long been my favorite way of eating leftover turkey for dinner (sandwiches being a lunchtime treat). These are good served with buttered steamed Brussels sprouts or broccoli.

¼ cup (½ stick) butter
½ cup all-purpose flour
2 cups milk
¼ teaspoon salt
¼ teaspoon freshly ground black pepper
3 tablespoons finely chopped parsley
3 scallions, white and green parts, finely chopped
5 cups finely chopped cooked turkey
1 teaspoon lemon juice
¼ teaspoon dried sage
½ teaspoon dried thyme
1 cup fine dry bread crumbs
2 large eggs, lightly beaten
Fat for deep frying

1. Melt the butter in a medium saucepan; then stir in the flour until well blended. Slowly stir in the milk and cook until the mixture thickens, about 5 minutes, stirring constantly. Season with salt and plenty of fresh pepper to taste.

2. Remove the sauce from heat and pour into a large mixing bowl. Add the parsley, scallions, turkey, lemon juice, sage, and thyme and blend well. Cover the bowl and chill until the mixture is firm, about 30 minutes.

3. Shape the croquette mixture into 10 squat cones, roll in bread crumbs, dip into the beaten eggs, and then roll in bread crumbs again. Place on a platter and allow to dry about 10 minutes at room temperature.

4. Fry in hot fat (about 375°F.) for about 5 minutes, or until golden brown, turning occasionally. Drain on paper towels and serve immediately.

COOKIES FOR SANTA

•

A BAKER'S DOZEN

Chocolate Buckeyes

Chocolate–Mint Bars

Philadelphia Raisin Squares

Great-Grandmother Floyd's Vanilla Horns

Grandma Stapleton's Bohemian Butter Cookies

Tom Thumb Bars

Date and Almond Pinwheels

Sylvia Barnes's Cardamom Icebox Cookies

My Favorite Oatmeal Cookies

Peanut Butter and Jelly Cookies

Butternut Balls

Betty Lou's Pecan Toffee Bars

Spicy Carrot Cookies

"Hang the merry
   garlands
Over all the town.
Smell the spicy odors
Of cookies turning
   brown!
The mice have
   come to nibble,
They're feeling
   mighty gay—
But only little
   children
Shall have my
   sweets today!"
Anonymous

*B*oth of my grandmothers were excellent bakers, and some of my earliest memories are of standing by their side, "helping," and eagerly waiting for the big moment when I could lick spatulas and bowls. Grandma Wynn lived with us for a time on the Ohio farm where I grew up, and on the first Saturday of December after my brothers, my sister, and I finished our chores, she would gather us into the big farmhouse kitchen to help bake and decorate cookies for Christmas. We would make dozens and dozens, and then fill huge 10-gallon lard cans with them, not stopping until a thousand cookies were baked and packed away. Every cookie was counted under Grandma's watchful eye, and not one could be eaten until Christmas Eve, when a few could be sampled with a glass of cold milk while preparing a plateful for Santa Claus.

These are old-fashioned cookies, easy recipes that have been passed along by loving hands, and they, along with the wonderful, communal cookie-baking experience, give me a warm sense of well-being.

Additional cookie recipes appear elsewhere in this book, as parts of menus (Gingerbread Kids, page 80; Chocolate Praline Lace Cookies, page 197; and Hazelnut Macaroons, page 94).

Getting Ready: This is a big job, and easier and a lot more fun when done with a few family members or friends. Of course the children should be put in charge of decorating the butter cookies.

A good shopping list is the best way to start out. As so many ingredients (especially flour, butter, and sugar) are repeated over and over, be sure to check your recipes and add up the ingredients to make sure you have enough of everything. It's no fun having to run to the grocery store and stand on a line just because you need a teaspoon of vanilla.

Make any cookie doughs that need to be chilled first (the Date and Almond Pinwheels, for example), and mix the drop cookies last. When you're ready to start baking, bake the cookies that require the same oven temperature in succession, so you don't have to wait for the oven to heat up or cool down.

Of course, the cookies don't all have to be made in one day, but I like to get this project done all in a weekend. If making the cookies more than a month before using them, freeze them, tightly wrapped.

"The best Christmas gift one can bestow on a child or a friend is a happy memory."
The New York Times, December 23, 1894

Chocolate Buckeyes

MAKES ABOUT 3 DOZEN COOKIES

Not quite cookies and not quite candies, these chocolate-covered peanutty morsels from the Buckeye State have been favorites of Ohioans for generations.

½ cup (1 stick) butter
¾ cup chunky peanut butter
1 cup graham cracker crumbs
1½ cups confectioners' sugar
1½ cups semisweet chocolate chips
2 tablespoons butter

1. Place ½ cup butter and the peanut butter in a small heavy-bottomed saucepan and place over low heat. Stir until melted and blended. Remove from heat.

2. Blend the graham cracker crumbs and confectioners' sugar together in a small mixing bowl; then gradually stir this mixture into the melted peanut butter mixture, mixing well to form a stiff dough.

3. In the top of a double boiler over simmering water, melt the chocolate chips and 2 tablespoons butter together. While this mixture is melting, form the dough into balls about 1 inch in diameter.

4. Spear the dough balls on the end of a toothpick and dip them into the melted chocolate mixture to coat two-thirds of each ball, leaving circles about the size of a penny uncoated. Place the coated balls on wax paper or aluminum foil and chill to set.

5. Pack the buckeyes in a tightly covered container lined with wax paper or aluminum foil and store in a cool, dry place.

Chocolate-Mint Bars

MAKES 3 DOZEN COOKIES

My Great-Aunt Susie made these whenever we went to visit her in Cleveland—the "big city." I always used to think of these as pretty sophisticated cookies, and I still do. These should be made no more than a week ahead.

½ cup (1 stick) butter
2 ounces unsweetened chocolate
¾ cup granulated sugar
2 large eggs
½ teaspoon peppermint extract
½ cup all-purpose flour
⅔ cup chopped walnuts

1. Preheat the oven to 350°F. Grease a 9-inch square cake pan.

2. Place the butter and chocolate in a small heavy saucepan and melt over low heat. Stir to blend and remove from heat. Beat in the sugar, then the eggs.

3. Add the peppermint extract and stir to combine. Add the flour, and mix well; then fold in the nuts.

4. Pour into the prepared pan and bake for about 25 minutes, or until a toothpick inserted in the center comes out clean. Cool in the pan before frosting.

Frosting
3 tablespoons butter
1 tablespoon milk
1 cup confectioners' sugar
1 teaspoon peppermint extract
1 ounce unsweetened chocolate

1. Blend 2 tablespoons of the butter and the milk together in a small mixing bowl. Beat in the sugar, then beat in the extract.

2. Spread this mixture over the cooled baked layer.

3. When the white icing is firm, melt the chocolate and the remaining tablespoon of butter together in a small heavy saucepan and combine well. Spread this mixture evenly over the white icing.

4. Cover the pan with aluminum foil or plastic wrap and chill until the chocolate frosting is firm. Cut into bars about 1 × 2¼ inches. Store in the refrigerator, tightly covered, up to one week.

Philadelphia Raisin Squares

MAKES ABOUT 3 DOZEN COOKIES

"Cookies for Santa"

●

Don't forget to put a plateful of your home-made cookies and a glass of milk for Santa when he makes his annual visit. After all, Santa loves cookies as much as you love presents. This custom comes from the Pennsylvania Dutch, who originated the tradition of Christmas cookies.

Santa as we know him in America today is the sum total of several from around the world, but this jolly old gentleman in a red suit began as St. Nicholas, the Bishop of Myra in Asia Minor during the first half of the fourth century, who gave away a fortune to the poor. The red and white of our modern Santa's suit are derived from the colors of his vestments.

The present form of "St. Nick" comes largely from the description in Clement Clarke Moore's *A Visit from St. Nicholas* (*'Twas the Night Before Christmas . . .*), written in 1822 as a Christmas poem for his children. Later in the nineteenth century, cartoonist Thomas Nast drew numerous cartoons of the round and rosy-cheeked Santa, firmly establishing his appearance.

Why is Santa so chubby? It's from eating a plateful of cookies in every house he visits on Christmas Eve!

⅓ cup butter, softened
⅓ cup firmly packed dark brown sugar
1 cup all-purpose flour
½ cup dark raisins
½ cup chopped walnuts
8 ounces cream cheese, softened
¼ cup granulated sugar
1 large egg
2 tablespoons milk
1 tablespoon lemon juice
½ teaspoon vanilla extract

1. Preheat the oven to 350°F.

2. In a large mixing bowl, cream together the butter and brown sugar; then blend in the flour, raisins, and walnuts. Set aside 1 cup of this mixture.

3. Pack the remainder of the mixture in an even layer in the bottom of a greased 8-inch square cake pan. Bake for 15 minutes, or until golden around the edges. Remove from the oven and cool on a wire rack.

4. While the crust is cooling, cream the cream cheese together with the granulated sugar, then add the remaining ingredients, beating until smooth.

5. Spread the cream cheese mixture over the cooled crust; then sprinkle the reserved mixture from step 1 over the surface.

6. Return the pan to the oven and bake for 30 minutes, or until the center is set. Remove from the oven and set the pan on a wire rack to cool.

7. Cut into 36 squares, and store in the refrigerator, tightly covered.

Great-Grandmother Floyd's Vanilla Horns

MAKES ABOUT 6 DOZEN COOKIES

⅔ cup confectioners' sugar
1 cup (2 sticks) butter
¾ cup ground blanched almonds
2 cups all-purpose flour
1½ teaspoons vanilla extract
Pinch of salt
Confectioners' sugar

1. Preheat the oven to 325°F.

2. Cream the sugar and butter together in a large mixing bowl. Slowly blend in the ground almonds; then blend in the flour. Add the vanilla and salt and mix the dough well.

3. To shape the dough into horns, pull off a piece of dough about the size of a walnut. Roll the dough between your palms to form a cylinder about ¼ inch in diameter. Shape the tube into a semicircle. Repeat, and place the horns about 1½ inches apart on a lightly buttered baking sheet.

4. Bake the cookies about 10 minutes, or until very lightly browned. Cool on wire racks and then roll the cookies in confectioners' sugar. Store at room temperature, tightly covered, for up to a month; or wrap tightly and freeze for up to 6 months.

Lunch for the Busy Bakers

●

With all the hubbub in the kitchen on cookie baking day, you certainly don't want to spend a whole lot of time cooking. I like to have tomato soup (yes, made from a can diluted with milk, not water, but still one of the great comfort foods) and toasted cheese or toasted peanut butter and banana sandwiches—lunch in a jiffy.

Grandma Stapleton's Bohemian Butter Cookies

MAKES 3 TO 4 DOZEN COOKIES,
DEPENDING ON COOKIE CUTTERS

This butter cookie recipe, brought to America by my great-grandmother, is perfect for making traditional Christmas shapes: bells, reindeer, stars, hearts, and trees. When I was a kid we all had our favorite cookie cutters. Mine was the large Santa Claus, so I decorated all of the Santas, leaving the other shapes to my brothers and sister.

1 cup sugar
2 cups (4 sticks) butter
4 large eggs
1 teaspoon vanilla extract
4 cups all-purpose flour
Assorted colored sugars for decoration

1. In a large mixing bowl, cream the butter and sugar together until light and smooth. Separate 3 of the eggs; beat the 3 egg yolks and the remaining whole egg into the butter-sugar mixture. Reserve the egg whites.

2. Beat in the vanilla; then gradually add the flour and mix well. Gather the dough into a ball, wrap in plastic wrap, and chill in the refrigerator for 3 hours or overnight.

3. Preheat the oven to 350°F. Grease baking sheets.

4. On a floured surface, roll out the dough to a thickness of ⅛ inch. Cut out shapes with floured cookie cutters. Transfer the cookies to baking sheets.

5. Lightly beat the egg whites. Using a pastry brush, glaze the surfaces of the cookies with the egg whites. Decorate each cookie with a sprinkling of colored sugar.

6. Bake for 8 to 10 minutes, or until the edges of the cookies are lightly browned. Remove to wire racks to cool.

7. Store in tightly covered containers for up to 2 months in a cool place, or freeze for up to 6 months.

Tom Thumb Bars

MAKES ABOUT 4 DOZEN COOKIES

½ cup (1 stick) butter
½ teaspoon salt
1½ cups firmly packed dark brown sugar
1 cup sifted all-purpose flour
1 teaspoon vanilla extract
2 large eggs
2 tablespoons all-purpose flour
½ teaspoon baking powder
1½ cups shredded coconut
1 cup coarsely chopped walnuts

1. Preheat the oven to 325°F. In a small mixing bowl, cream together the butter, salt, and ½ cup of the brown sugar; then blend in the sifted flour.

2. Spread the dough evenly in the bottom of a greased 8 × 12-inch cake pan with straight sides. Bake for 15 minutes, or until lightly browned. Remove from oven.

3. Beat together the remaining cup of brown sugar, vanilla, and eggs until foamy and thick; then beat in the 2 tablespoons flour and baking powder. Stir in the coconut and walnuts.

4. Spread this mixture over the surface of the prebaked layer; then return the pan to the oven and bake about 25 minutes longer, or until the surface is browned. Remove from the oven and cool in the pan on a wire rack. Cut into bars, 1 × 2 inches. Store at room temperature in a tightly covered container.

Chocolate Chip Tom Thumbs Fold ¾ cup semisweet chocolate chips into the dough at the end of step 1.

" 'Tis an ill cook that cannot lick his own fingers."
Shakespeare

Date and Almond Pinwheels

*T*ry dunking these into a glass of cold milk.

2½ cups chopped dried dates
1 cup granulated sugar
1 cup water
1 cup coarsely chopped almonds
1 cup (2 sticks) butter, softened
2 cups firmly packed dark brown sugar
3 eggs, beaten
4 cups sifted all-purpose flour
½ teaspoon salt
½ teaspoon baking soda

1. Combine the dates, granulated sugar, and water in a medium saucepan and cook over low heat until thick and syrupy, about 10 minutes. Stir in the almonds and set aside to cool.

2. Cream the butter and brown sugar together. Add the beaten eggs and beat well. Sift the flour, salt, and baking soda together and blend into the butter, brown sugar, and egg mixture. Form into a ball, wrap in plastic wrap, and chill thoroughly.

3. Divide the chilled dough ball into two even sections and roll each one out into a 9 x 12-inch rectangle about ¼ inch thick. Divide the date-nut mixture evenly between the dough rectangles and spread evenly. Roll each long piece up like a jelly roll. Chill the rolls thoroughly overnight.

4. Preheat the oven to 400°F. Remove the rolls from the refrigerator and cut them into ¼-inch-thick slices. Place the slices about 1 inch apart on greased baking sheets.

5. Bake the cookies for 10 to 12 minutes, or until lightly browned. Remove the wire racks to cool. Store in tightly covered containers in the refrigerator.

Sylvia Barnes's
Cardamom Icebox Cookies

MAKES ABOUT 5 DOZEN COOKIES

1 cup (2 sticks) butter
¾ cup granulated sugar
¾ cup firmly packed light brown sugar
3 large eggs, beaten
1 cup chopped walnuts
4 cups all-purpose flour
1 teaspoon salt
1½ teaspoons baking soda
1 tablespoon ground cardamom
Red and green colored sugars

1. Cream the butter and sugars together in a medium mixing bowl; beat in the eggs, then fold in the walnuts.

2. In a separate bowl, sift together the flour, salt, baking soda, and cardamom. Beat this into the butter-sugar-egg mixture, forming a stiff dough.

3. Divide the dough into quarters and shape into logs about 1¼ inches in diameter. Roll each log in wax paper and chill for several hours, or until firm enough to slice. (Cookies can be made ahead to this point and frozen tightly wrapped in aluminum foil.)

4. Preheat the oven to 375°F. Grease baking sheets.

5. Remove the dough logs from the refrigerator and roll them in colored sugar. Cut into ¼-inch-thick slices and place about 2 inches apart on greased baking sheets.

6. Bake about 10 minutes, or until the cookies are lightly browned. Remove to wire racks to cool; then store in tightly covered containers in a cool place.

Cinnamon Icebox Cookies Substitute cinnamon for the cardamom. (If making both versions, roll the cinnamon cookies in red sugar and cardamom cookies in green sugar for easy identification.)

My Favorite Oatmeal Cookies

MAKES ABOUT 6 DOZEN COOKIES

1 cup all-purpose flour
½ teaspoon baking soda
1 teaspoon ground cinnamon
¼ teaspoon salt
1 cup (2 sticks) butter
¾ cup firmly packed dark brown sugar
¼ cup granulated sugar
1 large egg
1 teaspoon vanilla extract
⅓ cup milk
2½ cups quick-cooking oats
½ cup chopped walnuts
1 cup chopped dried apricots

1. Preheat the oven to 375°F. Grease baking sheets.

2. Sift together the flour, baking soda, cinnamon, and salt.

3. In a separate large mixing bowl, cream the butter and sugars together; then beat in the egg. Beat in the vanilla and milk.

4. Stir the dry ingredients into the butter-sugar mixture, stirring until well blended. Fold in the oats, nuts, and apricots.

5. Drop the dough by teaspoonfuls onto the prepared baking sheets approximately 2 inches apart. Bake about 12 minutes, or until the edges of the cookies are browned. With a spatula, remove the cookies to a wire rack. When cool, store in tightly covered tins in a cool place.

"Alas! how dreary would be the world if there were no Santa Claus!...There would be no childlike faith, then, no poetry, no romance to make tolerable this existence....No Santa Claus! Thank God he lives, and lives forever."
Francis P. Church
New York Sun, 1897

Peanut Butter and Jelly Cookies

MAKES ABOUT 2½ DOZEN COOKIES

If you think you're too old for a peanut butter and jelly sandwich, just try one of these with a glass of cold milk and you'll be hooked —a kid again. Kids love making these as much as they like eating them. Why do peanut butter cookies always have the crisscross pattern? I don't know, do you?

½ cup (1 stick) butter, softened
½ cup chunky peanut butter
¼ cup granulated sugar
¾ cup firmly packed dark brown sugar
1 large egg
½ teaspoon vanilla extract
1½ cups all-purpose flour
½ teaspoon baking soda
½ teaspoon baking powder
¼ teaspoon salt
Strawberry jam

1. Preheat the oven to 350°F. Grease baking sheets.

2. In a mixing bowl, cream together the butter and peanut butter; then blend in both sugars. Add the egg and vanilla and mix well.

3. In a separate bowl, sift together the flour, baking soda, baking powder, and salt; then beat this mixture into the peanut butter mixture until smooth.

4. With lightly floured hands shape the dough into balls slightly less than 1 inch in diameter. Place the dough balls about 2 inches apart on the prepared baking sheets; then press them flat with the tines of a fork to make a crisscross pattern. With your thumb, make a depression in the center of each cookie. Fill each depression with about ½ teaspoon strawberry jam.

5. Bake for about 8 to 10 minutes, or until the cookies are lightly browned. With a spatula remove the cookies to wire racks. When cool, store them in tightly covered containers in a cool place.

Butternut Balls

MAKES ABOUT 5 DOZEN COOKIES

*T*hese are especially pretty Christmas cookies that don't require tedious decorating. They're even pretty without the candied cherries.

1 cup (2 sticks) butter, softened
¾ cup sugar
2 large eggs, separated
½ teaspoon vanilla extract
1 teaspoon grated orange rind
2¾ cups all-purpose flour
2 cups finely chopped butternuts *or* pecans
Halved red and green candied cherries

1. Preheat the oven to 325°F. Grease baking sheets.

2. Cream the butter and sugar together; then beat in the egg yolks, vanilla, and orange rind. Beat in the flour until well combined and a stiff dough is formed.

3. Form the dough into small balls about ¾ inch in diameter. Lightly beat the egg whites in a small bowl. Dip the balls into the egg whites; then dip them into the chopped nuts, coating about three-quarters of each ball. Place the dough balls, uncoated side down, about 2 inches apart on the prepared baking sheets. Press a candied cherry half into the top of each ball, flattening the ball slightly.

4. Bake the cookies for about 25 minutes, or until lightly browned and a toothpick inserted into a cookie comes out clean. Cool on wire racks and store in a tightly covered container in a cool place.

Betty Lou's Pecan Toffee Bars

MAKES ABOUT 3 DOZEN COOKIES

1 cup (2 sticks) butter, softened
1 cup firmly packed light brown sugar
1 large egg
1 teaspoon vanilla extract
1¾ cups all-purpose flour
8 ounces semisweet chocolate
¾ cup finely chopped pecans

1. Preheat the oven to 350°F. Grease a shallow rectangular cake pan approximately 10½ × 14½ inches.

2. Cream together the butter and brown sugar; then beat in the egg and vanilla. Beat in the flour until well blended. Spread the dough evenly in the pan and bake for 35 to 40 minutes, or until the surface is lightly browned.

3. When the cookies are almost finished baking, melt the chocolate in the top of a double boiler or a small heavy saucepan over medium heat. When the cookies are baked, spread the melted chocolate in an even layer over the surface; then sprinkle on a layer of chopped nuts.

4. Cool in the pan for 15 minutes; then cut into bars approximately 1 × 2 inches and place them on a wire rack to cool completely. Store in tightly covered containers in a cool place.

The Absolute Best Chocolate Chip Cookies

●

By now, you've probably noticed that this chapter does *not* include a recipe for America's favorite, the chocolate chip cookie. Volumes have been written about which is the best chocolate chip cookie. Whether it's one of David's Cookies, one of Famous Amos's famous ones, Chips Ahoy, or your Great-Aunt Tillie's secret recipe, let the controversy end here. As Dorothy found in *The Wizard of Oz*, the thing you've been looking for is right in your own backyard, or more precisely, on the back of the Nestle's chocolate chip package.

Yes, the original Toll House Cookie is still the best. (Though I have to admit I have, on occasion, substituted all brown sugar for the brown sugar and white sugar called for—just drop the dough a bit farther apart on the baking sheet, as these spread a bit more). Enough said!

Spicy Carrot Cookies

MAKES ABOUT 6 DOZEN COOKIES

These easy drop cookies are made with all the good things found in carrot cake: spices, raisins, nuts, and, of course, carrots. Make them at least a week before serving to allow flavors to develop.

½ cup (1 stick) butter
1 cup firmly packed dark brown sugar
¼ cup granulated sugar
1 large egg
½ teaspoon vanilla extract
1 teaspoon grated orange rind
2¼ cups all-purpose flour
½ teaspoon baking soda
1 teaspoon baking powder
½ teaspoon salt
2½ teaspoons ground cinnamon
2 teaspoons ground ginger
1 teaspoon grated nutmeg
1½ cups finely grated raw carrot
1 cup shredded coconut
1 cup chopped walnuts
1 cup golden raisins
Confectioners' sugar

1. Preheat the oven to 375°F. Grease baking sheets.

2. In a large mixing bowl, cream together the butter and sugars; then beat in the egg, vanilla, and orange rind.

3. In a separate bowl, sift together the flour, baking soda, baking powder, salt, and spices. Gradually stir this mixture into the butter mixture and blend well. Fold in the carrot, coconut, walnuts, and raisins.

4. Drop the dough by teaspoonfuls onto the prepared baking sheets, about 2 inches apart. Bake for 10 to 12 minutes, or until the cookies are golden brown.

5. Remove the cookies to wire racks and cool; then dust with confectioners' sugar. Pack the cookies in tightly covered containers with a slice of apple or orange to keep them moist. Store in a cool place up to a month (do not freeze).

A TREE-TRIMMING BUFFET DINNER

•

FOR 8 TO 10

MENU

Mulled Beaujolais Nouveau

Assorted Cheeses and Crackers

"Quick" Cassoulet

Watercress and Arugula Salad

Apple–Ginger Sorbet

Grandmother Stapleton's Bohemian

Butter Cookies (page 55)

*E*very year around the second week in December, *The New York Times* runs a list of Christmas tree farms within easy driving distance of the metropolitan area where you can chop down your own tree. And each year, a group of us pile into the car and go off on our search for the perfect tree. We have done it in rainstorms, blizzards, and when the temperature has dipped to 5 degrees below zero—nothing deters our mission.

One very cold and very gray Saturday in December a few years ago, our quest took us to eastern Pennsylvania, and we visited three farms before finding the perfect trees. We chopped down five trees, as we were bringing back trees for other family members and friends, and after a lengthy struggle and much maneuvering, got them tied onto the roof and sides of my Volkswagen Beetle. As

"Nothing that is blue, gold, silver, pink or any other color other than green is a Christmas tree."

Andy Rooney

"One can never be too rich, too thin, or have too many ornaments on one's Christmas tree."

Anonymous

64

Tree-Trimming Ideas
●

Old Times For an old-fashioned, down-home tree, use colored lights, popcorn, and cranberry garlands, and paper chains made of loops of brightly colored paper. Cut out colorful, old-fashioned pictures and tie them onto the tree with red yarn. Finish the tree by draping the branches with old-fashioned tinsel.

Winter Wonderland For a formal and dramatic tree, use miniature white lights, silvery and clear glass ornaments of all shapes and sizes, cut-paper snowflakes, ropes of silver glass beads, and clear glass icicles.

Country Christmas Use white lights and strings of popcorn and cranberries. Tie cookie animals, gingerbread boys and girls, cornhusk dolls, tiny red and green apples, and pine cones onto the branches with red gingham ribbons.

Formal Victorian Use miniature pink lights, big purple and pink velvet and lace bows, lacy white fans made from paper doilies, pink satin balls, and big sprigs of baby's breath.

Flower Fantasy Start early in the year and collect flowers that dry well. Use them with big burgundy and gold satin bows, miniature yellow lights, and sprigs of dried bittersweet.

we ventured onto the highway, we looked like a small traveling forest, and we could barely see out of the windows through the overhanging evergreen branches. And then it began to snow. . . .

Putting up the tree and decorating it can be far less hazardous and almost as much fun, especially with a group of family and friends joining in. There is a never-ending joy when unwrapping each Christmas tree ornament every year, marveling at it all over again, and remembering where it came from. City living does not allow some of my friends space for a large Christmas tree, so they are invited to share our tree. Tree-trimming night, usually a week-night, is also the official night in our house to bring out the Christmas albums and tapes.

Since this menu is a buffet, I serve it right from the kitchen, allowing the tree-trimmers to eat and work at their own pace; this also keeps some of the mess out of the living room, which is already filled with tree-trimmers and boxes of ornaments. Serve dessert after the last ornament is in place on the tree, and sit back and admire the view.

Getting Ready: Because the focus of this evening is tree-trimming and not cooking, everything is prepared ahead, except for the tossing of the salad, which takes only a minute. This makes this menu perfect to serve on a weeknight right after work.

The syrup for the mulled wine can be made several days ahead and stored in the refrigerator. Warm it up half an hour before serving and add the wine.

The cassoulet is easy to make ahead and tastes even better if given a day or two to mellow. Reheat it for one hour in a moderate oven. A pungent, crunchy watercress and arugula salad can hold its own against a hearty cassoulet. Tear two cups each of watercress and arugula and one head of Boston lettuce into bite-size pieces. In a jar, combine one-quarter cup each walnut oil, olive oil, red wine vinegar, and chopped walnuts with a pinch of sugar and dry mustard and salt and pepper to taste. Cover, shake well, and toss with the greens just before serving. The sorbet can be made and frozen several weeks before serving. The cookies are from your Christmas cookie stockpile, so there's no fuss here, either.

Have the tree in its stand with the top ornament and the lights in place before your guests arrive. In our house, Freddy the stuffed mouse is the first thing to go on the tree, so he, too, can enjoy the proceedings from his perch on top of the tree. Have your ornament boxes arranged in the general order in which you want the ornaments to go onto the tree. After the lights, I like to put on the glass ornaments toward the inside of the tree, followed by the beads, and then all the wooden and ceramic ornaments. The final touch is hundreds of glass icicles on the tips of each branch.

Setting: The tree is the star and the buffet is set in the kitchen, so there's no need for a table setting. Use informal dishes, flatware, and napkins, and serve the mulled wine in heavy mugs.

Beverages: For those who prefer a cold drink, serve a chilled Beaujolais Nouveau or hard cider, or even a cold, light beer, with the meal. Hot espresso with coffee liqueur goes well with dessert.

Mulled Beaujolais Nouveau

MAKES ABOUT 20 SERVINGS

What a wonderful drink this is to serve on a cold evening—it's so warm, friendly, and comforting. The syrup base can be made several days in advance and reheated just before serving.

8 unpeeled medium oranges, coarsely chopped
1 cup sugar
1 teaspoon grated nutmeg
1 teaspoon ground cinnamon
1 tablespoon whole cloves
6 cups water
3 bottles Beaujolais Nouveau
Small apples studded with whole cloves
Cinnamon sticks

1. Combine the first 5 ingredients with the water in a medium saucepan and bring to a simmer. Cover the pan and simmer gently for 30 minutes. Remove from heat and cool.

2. Strain the syrup through a double layer of cheesecloth, transfer to a covered jug, and refrigerate until ready to use.

3. About half an hour before serving, bring the syrup to a boil in a large stockpot. Remove from heat and stir in the wine. Warm it up again, but do not allow the mixture to simmer. Add the apples studded with cloves to the pot while reheating.

4. To serve, ladle directly from the pot into warmed mugs garnished with cinnamon sticks.

"Quick" Cassoulet

This recipe does not take as little time as some recipes for a streamlined cassoulet, but there is only so far cassoulet can be pared down and still have a resemblance to the original. There are a lot of steps here, but this is not really a difficult dish to make. This is a super-hearty dish—hope for a cold night and big appetites!

1 pound dried Great Northern beans
½ pound lean salt pork *or* slab bacon
4 1-inch-thick pork loin chops
4 1-inch-thick lamb loin chops
1 pound garlic sausage *or* kielbasa
1 turkey drumstick, roasted
3 medium onions, coarsely chopped
6 large garlic cloves, chopped
½ cup dry white wine
3 cups crushed canned Italian plum tomatoes
1 teaspoon dried thyme
1 teaspoon dried basil
½ cup chopped parsley
3 bay leaves
Salt and freshly ground black pepper
½ cup fresh dry bread crumbs
3 to 4 tablespoons butter, melted
Parsley sprigs

1. Pick over the beans and rinse well. Place in a large saucepan with water to cover. Place the pan on the stove and bring to a boil. Turn off the heat, cover the pan, and allow the beans to soak for 1 hour.

2. Cut the salt pork or bacon into ¼-inch cubes. If using salt pork, place in a small saucepan with water to cover and blanch for 5 minutes to remove excess salt; then drain. Place the salt pork or bacon in a 4-quart Dutch oven and sauté over medium heat, stirring occasionally, until translucent and the fat is well rendered, about 10 minutes. Remove the cubes from the pan with a slotted spoon and reserve. Remove all but 3 tablespoons fat from the pan and reserve.

3. While the salt pork or bacon is sautéing, cut the meat from the pork chops and lamb chops off the bone and cut it into ¾-inch chunks. Reserve the bones. Cut the sausage on the diagonal into ½-inch slices.

4. Add the pork and lamb chunks to the Dutch oven and toss with the rendered fat. Sauté until lightly browned, about 10 minutes.

67

The Christmas Tree

•

One of our most popular Christmas traditions, which most of us think of as the very essence of Christmas in Victorian England, is neither English nor Victorian. The tradition of a decorated evergreen tree at Christmas time is believed to go back to the fifteenth or sixteenth century in Germany's Upper Rhine Valley. Later, it seems that England's Queen Charlotte, the wife of George IV, had a Christmas tree long before Prince Albert—Victoria's consort, who is often credited with England's first Christmas tree—ever appeared on the scene.

The first Christmas tree in the United States is credited to a twenty-one-year-old Bavarian immigrant named August Imgard. Missing the customs of his homeland, he erected a Christmas tree on December 24, 1847, in his new home in Wooster, Ohio. A lighted tree is erected every year in Wooster at August Imgard's tomb to commemorate his contribution to America's Christmas tradition.

5. Cut the meat from the turkey drumstick, including skin, and cut it into ¾-inch chunks. Reserve the bone. Add the turkey chunks to the Dutch oven along with the sliced sausage, and sauté all the meats for 5 minutes, tossing occasionally. Remove the browned meats from the Dutch oven with a slotted spoon and reserve.

6. Add enough reserved fat to the Dutch oven to make 3 tablespoons. Add the chopped onion and garlic, and sauté until golden, about 7 minutes. Add the wine, raise the heat, and simmer for 5 minutes, scraping all brown bits from the bottom of the pan.

7. Add the tomatoes, herbs, and reserved bones to the pan. Bring to a simmer, lower the heat, cover, and simmer for 30 minutes, stirring occasionally. The sauce should be fairly thick.

8. Preheat the oven to 325°F. Remove the bones from the sauce and discard them. Season the sauce with salt and freshly ground black pepper to taste. Do not oversalt—the salt pork will add saltiness to the finished cassoulet. The sauce should otherwise be strongly seasoned.

9. Return the meats to the Dutch oven. Drain the beans and reserve the liquid; then add the beans to the Dutch oven. Stir the mixture well to combine the sauce and beans and distribute the beans. Sprinkle the bread crumbs over the surface and drizzle the melted butter onto the crumbs.

10. Place the casserole in the oven and bake, uncovered, for 2 hours, or until the beans are tender and the top is well browned. Check periodically during baking and, if the casserole seems to be too dry, add a bit of reserved bean liquid. Serve hot, garnished with parsley sprigs.

Apple-Ginger Sorbet

MAKES 2 QUARTS

Tree-Trimming Ideas

•

Kitchen Tree Decorate a small tree with lemons and limes studded with cloves; hollowed-out eggshells; bunches of cinnamon sticks tied up in red ribbon; and shiny cookie cutters, small whisks, and other small shiny utensils, all tied on with red and green ribbons.

Jingle Bells Tie clusters of silvery jingle bells together with red plaid ribbon to decorate a small tree and add twinkling miniature white lights, holly sprigs, and bunches of pine cones.

Tree of Gold Decorate the tree using shiny and matte gold balls of all sizes, fans made from gold foil, miniature white lights, and sprigs of baby's breath, all accented with small red velvet bows.

Far East Fantasy Use tiny red lights and paper lanterns, small Oriental dolls and masks, and multicolored Oriental paper fans.

Memory Tree Whenever I travel, I try to pick up some small souvenir object to hang on the tree and scout antiques shops and flea markets for antique ornaments. As the collection gets bigger, it's fun to remember each year where each ornament came from.

1½ cups sugar
¾ cup water
¾ cup cider *or* apple juice
¼ teaspoon ground cinnamon
1 teaspoon ground ginger
6 large tart apples
¼ cup lemon juice
½ cup Calvados *or* applejack
Calvados
Chopped candied ginger

1. Combine the sugar, water, and cider in a saucepan and place over medium heat. Stir until the sugar dissolves and bubbles begin to form in the bottom of the pan. Remove from heat and pour into a large mixing bowl. Stir in the spices and chill about 20 minutes.

2. While the syrup is chilling, peel and core the apples and chop coarsely; then puree with the lemon juice in the bowl of a food processor fitted with the steel chopping blade.

3. Remove the syrup from the refrigerator and stir in the Calvados or applejack and pureed apples. Pour the mixture into an ice-cream maker and follow the manufacturer's instructions, *or* continue with step 4.

4. Pour the mixture into a large metal pan (a rectangular cake pan is ideal) and place in the freezer. When ice crystals begin to form, about 30 minutes, remove from the freezer and beat the mixture until smooth. Return the pan to the freezer and repeat this process two or three times, or until a smooth, firm, finely grained consistency has been reached.

5. About 30 minutes before serving, transfer the sorbet from the freezer to the refrigerator to allow it to soften slightly. At serving time, scoop into wineglasses. Top each serving with 1 tablespoon Calvados and a sprinkling of chopped candied ginger.

WASSAILING BUFFET SUPPER

•

FOR 20

MENU

Mulled Cider Wassail Bowl

Onion–Rosemary Tartlets

Country Thyme Pâté   Spinach Pesto Pâté

Assorted Cheese and Sausages with Mustards

Assorted Breads and Crackers   Popcorn

Homemade Cookies   Fresh Winter Fruits

*W*hen I was about fourteen, we moved from the farm into town, and one of my favorite memories of living in the small town of Willard, Ohio, is when my family and friends would gather on a night just before Christmas and venture onto the streets to go caroling. Now my extended family in New York City has revived this happy tradition, after which we bring our cold bodies and warm souls indoors to this simple and hearty indoor picnic, where the caroling continues.

Getting Ready: This menu, perfect for a weeknight, requires no last-minute preparation, because everything to be homemade can be done ahead and the rest of the menu is store-bought.

The cider and spices for the Mulled Cider Wassail Bowl can be combined several hours ahead of time and left to stand at room temperature. Turn the stove on at low heat and pour in the wine when you come back home from caroling.

"This ancient silver bowl of mine,
it tells of good old times,
Of joyous days, and jolly nights,
and merry Christmas chimes.
They were a free and jovial race,
but honest, brave and true
That dipped their ladle in the punch when this old bowl was new."
Oliver Wendell Holmes

70

The Onion–Rosemary Tartlets can be prepared ahead, and refrigerated, or the filling can be prepared ahead and frozen, and you can roll out the pastry and assemble them just before baking with the aid of a helper.

The Country Thyme Pâté can be made ahead and stored in the refrigerator for up to a week or made well in advance and frozen. The Spinach Pesto Pâté should not be frozen, but can be made a day or two in advance and refrigerated.

With the widespread availability of wonderful domestic and imported cheeses, this can be a true adventure in eating. Vary the cheeses according to texture, color, and intensity of flavor, based on the selection in your local market. Three or four different cheeses, attractively arranged in big hunks on a cutting board with three different sausages, make a nice array. For this menu, allow about one pound each of cheese and sausage for every six people. Place stoneware crocks of several different types of mustards on the board, too, along with several good knives.

With fresh bakery departments now in many supermarkets, serving excellent breads no longer means having to bake your own. Long loaves are perfect for this menu, so guests can just break off a hunk. If you use breads that require slicing with a knife, put them on a cutting board. Otherwise, arrange the breads in a big rustic basket lined with a napkin, and do likewise with a good assortment of crackers.

Fresh-popped popcorn takes only a few minutes to make in an electric popper. I serve it in an antique over-the-fire corn popper.

Take the sausages and cheeses out of the refrigerator and arrange them on a board, loosely covered, before you go out caroling so that they'll be at room temperature at serving time. Also arrange a big platter of your homemade cookies ahead of time.

Beverages: Cold beer and a good hearty red jug wine go very well with this menu. With dessert serve hot cocoa (page 81) garnished with marshmallows and candy canes (and maybe with a bit of Kahlua or crème de menthe stirred in).

Setting: I set up a table near the fireplace in my living room, and drape it with a green cloth. Several small, low poinsettia plants grouped in a big rustic basket serve as a centerpiece. If you have no fireplace, a grouping of fat red candles of varying heights on a wood cutting board will give the room the right kind of happy glow. Use baskets and boards for serving to go along with the "indoor picnic" mood.

"Be of Good Health"

•

The custom of wassailing is an old English one. Groups of friends would travel from house to house "a-wassailing" to wish their neighbors joy and good health during the holiday season and the coming years: "Wes hal!" — "Be of good health!" Afterward they would return to one of their homes to toast one another with a cup of hot punch consisting of ale or wine mulled with spices. Soon the term "wassail" referred to the delicious brew itself, as well as the happy "wassailing" excursions.

Mulled Cider Wassail Bowl

MAKES 40 TO 50 SERVINGS

The aroma of this spicy punch warming on the stove will let everyone know it's holiday time the minute they walk in the door. This drink should be served warm, so if your kitchen is easily accessible and large enough, you can let your guests help themselves right from the stove.

1 gallon freshly pressed apple cider
8 cinnamon sticks
1 tablespoon whole allspice
1 tablespoon whole cloves
1 orange, sliced horizontally
1 lemon, sliced horizontally
1 gallon good-quality dry white jug wine
2 cups light rum

1. Combine the cider, spices, and sliced fruit in a stockpot large enough to hold the wine and rum. Bring to almost a simmer and allow the mixture to mull for about 1 hour over very low heat.

2. About 10 minutes before serving, pour in the wine and rum, and stir to combine. Allow the mixture to heat, but do not allow it to come to the simmering point. Serve warm.

Onion-Rosemary Tartlets

MAKES ABOUT 6 DOZEN

These fragrant morsels are invariably a hit; they disappear almost as quickly as the platter is passed. Use only firm, good-quality red onions; if they are unavailable, substitute yellow onions. If any onion filling is left over, it can be frozen for later use.

½ cup (1 stick) butter
8 medium red onions, thinly sliced and separated into rings
10 to 12 scallions, white and green parts, sliced
1½ cups dry red wine
¾ cup red wine vinegar
½ teaspoon sugar
1½ teaspoons dried rosemary leaves
Salt and freshly ground black pepper
1 pound frozen puff pastry, thawed in refrigerator

1. Melt the butter in a Dutch oven or a large heavy saucepan. Add the onions and scallions and sauté over medium heat, stirring occasionally, for about 20 minutes, or until the onions soften and begin to brown.

2. Add the red wine, vinegar, sugar, and rosemary and simmer over low heat for about 30 minutes, or until the onions are very soft and most of the liquid has evaporated. Stir occasionally to prevent sticking. Season to taste with salt and plenty of freshly ground black pepper and remove from heat.

3. While the onions are cooking, prepare the pastry shells: Preheat the oven to 400°F. Cut the puff pastry into two even pieces. Roll out one piece on a well-floured board into a square about ⅛ inch thick, and about 14 inches square. Cut the pastry into 2-inch squares and press the squares into miniature muffin pans. Gently press the corners of the dough down onto the flat surface of the pan. Prick the bottoms and sides of the dough all around with a fork.

4. Using half of the onion mixture, fill each tartlet shell with about 2 teaspoonfuls of the mixture. This is most efficiently done with the fingers. Poke any stray onion strands into the tartlets. (May be assembled ahead and refrigerated or frozen, tightly wrapped, at this point.) Bake for 10 to 12 minutes, or until the pastry is puffed and golden brown.

5. Remove the tartlets to a baking sheet and keep warm. Using the remaining piece of pastry and the remaining onion mixture, prepare the remaining shells, fill and bake as above. Serve immediately, or, to bake ahead, continue with step 6.

6. Cover tightly with aluminum foil or plastic wrap and refrigerate. About 1 hour before serving, bring the tarts to room temperature, remove the covering, and heat in a preheated 325°F. oven for about 10 minutes.

Onion–Cheese Tartlets Sprinkle about ½ teaspoon grated Gruyère or Swiss cheese onto each filled tartlet before baking and you have onion soup gratinée—without the soup!

Onion–Mushroom Tartlets Substitute 1 pound coarsely chopped mushrooms for half the red onions. Use only ¼ cup vinegar and substitute tarragon for the rosemary.

Country Thyme Pâté

SERVES 20 TO 25 AS AN HORS D'OEUVRE
OR 8 TO 10 AS A FIRST COURSE

This thyme-scented pâté involves quite a few steps, but it's not at all difficult to make.

In addition to serving it as an hors d'oeuvre, try it as a first course, sliced and garnished with a dollop of Cranberry–Kumquat Compote (page 166). This pâté is best served at room temperature.

2½ tablespoons olive oil
½ cup chopped mushrooms
1 large onion, finely chopped
2 garlic cloves, finely chopped
¼ cup dry white wine
2 tablespoons brandy
1 teaspoon salt
1 teaspoon freshly ground black pepper
1 tablespoon chopped fresh thyme *or* 1 teaspoon dried thyme
¼ teaspoon ground allspice
¾ pound ground lean pork
¾ pound uncooked ground chicken *or* turkey breast
2 ounces ground pork fat
1 large egg, lightly beaten
¼ cup chopped parsley
About 1 pound thinly sliced bacon
Parsley *or* thyme sprigs

1. Preheat the oven to 375°F.

2. Combine the olive oil, mushrooms, onion, and garlic in a small skillet over medium heat and sauté until quite tender, about 15 minutes. Add the wine, brandy, salt, pepper, thyme, and allspice; bring to a boil. Lower the heat and simmer gently for 10 minutes. Remove to a large mixing bowl.

3. Add the pork, chicken or turkey, pork fat, egg, and parsley. Blend the mixture well with your hands until thoroughly combined.

4. Line the bottom and sides of an 8½ × 4½ × 2½-inch loaf pan with overlapping slices of bacon, letting the ends of the slices hang over the sides of the pan.

5. Pack the pâté mixture tightly into the bacon-lined pan and fold the overhanging slices over the top of the pâté mixture. Fill in any holes on top with additional slices of bacon.

6. Cover the pan tightly with aluminum foil and place in a larger baking pan. Fill the large pan with hot water to come halfway up the sides of the loaf pan. Place in the oven and bake for 1½ hours.

7. When the pâté is done, remove the loaf pan from the larger pan and cool on a wire rack. Weight the top of the pâté with full cans or jars and place in the refrigerator overnight. (The weights will firm and tighten the texture of the pâté.

8. When ready to serve, dip the pâté in a pan of warm water; then gently slip a knife around the sides of the pâté. Invert onto a cutting board or serving platter, and garnish with parsley or sprigs of fresh thyme.

"As well might we dance without music, or attempt to write a poem without rhythm, as to keep Christmas without a Christmas tree."
Weekly Press of Philadelphia, *1877*

Spinach Pesto Pâté

SERVES 20 AS AN HORS D'OEUVRE
OR 8 TO 10 AS A FIRST COURSE

2 large garlic cloves
1 cup loosely packed basil leaves
10 ounces chopped spinach, stems removed
1 cup coarse dry bread crumbs
4 large eggs
1 medium onion, quartered
1 teaspoon salt
¼ teaspoon grated nutmeg
¼ teaspoon freshly ground black pepper
1¼ cups ricotta cheese
¼ cup grated Parmesan cheese
4 to 5 large mushrooms
½ cup walnut pieces
1 large mushroom
4 whole spinach leaves, wilted

1. Preheat the oven to 350°F.

2. Toss the garlic cloves into a running food processor fitted with the metal chopping blade and mince them. Turn the processor off and add the basil leaves and spinach; then process until coarsely chopped.

3. Add the remaining ingredients, except one large mushroom and the wilted spinach leaves, to the processor bowl. Process until the mushrooms and walnuts are coarsely chopped and the mixture is well blended.

"Deck the Halls with . . ."

●

The *flora* used to decorate our tables and homes and that are traditionally symbolic of the Christmas season, are those which have long been available at this time of year.

Evergreens, such as pine, spruce, and balsam fir, are used to make garlands and wreaths.

Poinsettia, the "flower of the holy night," is an American Christmas symbol, brought to South Carolina in 1829 by Ambassador Joel R. Poinsett after his tenure in Mexico, where the Franciscan friars in Mexico had adorned their nativity celebrations with the red-leafed plant since the seventeenth century.

Holly and ivy have been used during the Christmas season in Britain for centuries. Holly was considered masculine and ivy feminine, and together they were thought to bring good luck and fertility during the coming year.

Mistletoe, a symbol of good luck and fertility and the plant of peace, was held sacred in ancient times. From its use as a fertility symbol, our custom of kissing "under the mistletoe" evolved.

Other traditional Christmas flora include the amaryllis, narcissus, and branches of quince and bittersweet.

4. Slice the remaining mushroom and arrange the perfect slices only in a row in the bottom of the greased pan. Use the wilted spinach leaves to line the bottom of the pan and come partially up the sides of the pan in an uneven pattern. Carefully spoon the pâté mixture into the pan so as not to disturb the leaves.

5. Bake for 1 hour, or until a toothpick or cake tester inserted into the center of the pâté comes out clean. Cool to room temperature and then chill.

6. To serve, dip the pâté pan into warm water and slide a blunt knife along the edge of the pâté to loosen it from the pan. Invert onto a cutting board or serving platter and serve with thinly sliced, toasted Italian bread or crackers.

A KIDS' LUNCHTIME PARTY

•

FOR 8

MENU

Toasted Cheese on Whole Wheat Sandwiches

Macaroni and Meatball Soup

Gingerbread Kids

Old-Fashioned Hot Cocoa with Candy Canes

Red and Green Apples

"Most all the time, the whole year round there ain't no flies on me, But jest 'fore Christmas I'm as good as I kin be!"
Eugene Field

*H*ere's a good meal to serve at a lunchtime holiday party for kids or adults, and part of the fun is the making of the Gingerbread Kids. If baking is not the main activity of the day, amuse the kids by playing musical chairs with Christmas songs as the music, or play "pin the red nose on Rudolph." This is also a good menu to serve on cookie baking day.

Getting Ready: The soup can be made ahead up to the point of adding the last few ingredients and simmering for 5 minutes. The cheese sandwiches can be assembled a few hours ahead, stored tightly wrapped in the refrigerator, and popped under the broiler about 10 minutes before serving. The making of the Gingerbread Kids can be either part of the festivities or done well ahead of time. The cocoa must be made just before serving, but it takes just a few minutes.

Setting: As a centerpiece arrange a pile of small, brightly wrapped inexpensive gifts, each marked "Do not open before Christmas," in a basket in the center of the table. Let one end of each ribbon extend to each place setting. At the end of the meal, let the children pull out their own gifts and open them up, despite the labeling, as a pre-Christmas treat.

Toasted Cheese on Whole Wheat Sandwiches

1. Preheat the broiler.

2. Lightly butter one side *each* of two slices of whole wheat bread for each sandwich then arrange half of the slices, buttered side down, on a baking sheet.

3. Layer several thick slices of cheese (Cheddar, Swiss, or mozzarella) onto the bread on the baking sheet; then top with the remaining bread, buttered sides up.

4. Place the baking sheet about 4 or 5 inches from the heat source in the broiler and cook until the surface of the bread is lightly toasted. Flip the sandwiches with a spatula, and toast the other side until browned. Serve immediately.

I usually like to make melted cheese sandwiches in butter in a skillet, but this method works best when making them for a crowd. Any number of other ingredients are wonderful layered onto the cheese before toasting the sandwiches. For the grown-ups, try roasted peppers, slivered sun-dried tomatoes in olive oil, sliced smoked turkey, ham, or sausages. For the kids of any age, toasted peanut butter and banana or peanut butter and bacon sandwiches are excellent made this way, too.

Macaroni and Meatball Soup

SERVES 8

Hearty and easy to make, this soup isn't just for kids; it makes a good lunch or supper main course for just about anyone.

1 pound ground beef chuck
½ cup fine dry bread crumbs
1 garlic clove, finely chopped
1 small onion, finely chopped
¼ cup grated Parmesan *or* Romano cheese
3 tablespoons chopped parsley
¼ teaspoon dried oregano
¼ teaspoon salt
¼ teaspoon freshly ground black pepper
1 large egg, lightly beaten
4 thick slices bacon, diced
2 garlic cloves, finely chopped
2 medium onions, coarsely chopped
1 large green pepper, diced
2 quarts well-seasoned beef stock
2 cups tomato puree
1 cup diced carrots
1 cup cooked white beans
½ cup chopped parsley
½ teaspoon dried oregano
8 ounces cut ziti *or* bowtie pasta, cooked *al dente*
Salt and freshly ground black pepper

1. Combine the first ten ingredients (up to and including the egg) in a medium mixing bowl and mix well with your hands. Shape the mixture into balls about ¾ inch in diameter.

2. Place the bacon in the bottom of a Dutch oven and sauté over medium heat until not quite crisp, about 7 minutes. Remove all but 3 tablespoons of fat.

3. Brown the meatballs, a few at a time, on all sides and reserve; then sauté the garlic, onion, and green pepper about 5 minutes.

4. Add the stock, tomato puree, carrots, and meatballs to the Dutch oven and bring to a boil over medium heat. Lower the heat and simmer until the carrots are tender, about 20 minutes. Add the white beans, parsley, oregano, and macaroni, and then simmer for 5 minutes longer. Season with salt and pepper and serve immediately.

"Christmas time is
coming,
The geese are
getting fat.
Please to put a
penny
In an old man's hat!
If you haven't got a
penny,
A ha'penny will do,
If you haven't got a
ha'penny,
God Bless you!"
Old Nursery Rhyme

Gingerbread Kids

MAKES ABOUT 2 DOZEN COOKIES,
DEPENDING ON THE SIZE OF CUTTER

If the dough for these Gingerbread Kids is made ahead you can bring it out and have the real kids help roll and cut it. Or make the cookies ahead and then let them jump in to decorate the cookies. These cookies keep well, stored in a tightly covered tin in a cool place, and they also make great gifts.

"I don't s'pose any-body on earth likes gingerbread better'n I do and gets less'n I do."
Abraham Lincoln

1 cup (2 sticks) butter, softened
1 cup firmly packed light brown sugar
¾ cup dark molasses
1 large egg, lightly beaten
5 cups all-purpose flour
1 teaspoon salt
1½ teaspoons baking powder
2 teaspoons ground ginger
1½ teaspoons ground cinnamon
1½ teaspoons ground cloves
½ teaspoon grated nutmeg
Dark raisins for decorating

1. In a large mixing bowl, cream the butter, sugar, and molasses together; then beat in the egg.

2. In a separate bowl, stir all the remaining ingredients except the raisins together with a fork until well blended; then beat this mixture into the butter-sugar mixture. Shape the dough into a ball, wrap it tightly in aluminum foil or plastic wrap, and chill until firm, about 3 hours.

3. Preheat the oven to 350°F. Grease baking sheets. Divide the dough into two parts. Return one half to the refrigerator and roll the other out on a floured surface to a thickness of a little less than ¼ inch. Cut out the cookies with a gingerbread man cookie cutter. Lightly press raisins into the dough to make eyes, noses, mouths, and buttons.

4. Using a wide, flat spatula, transfer the cookies to the baking sheets and bake until the edges of the cookies are lightly browned, 10 to 12 minutes. When done, remove the cookies to wire racks to cool before decorating.

5. Repeat steps 3 and 4 with the other half of the dough and then with the reserved trimmings. Decorate the cookies with the frosting.

Decorative Frosting
3 cups confectioners' sugar
2 egg whites
Food coloring

1. In a small mixing bowl, beat together the confectioners' sugar and egg whites to form a thick frosting. Add a few drops of water if necessary.

2. Divide the icing into four or five custard cups or very small bowls and color each with a few drops of food coloring, beating with a fork. Pipe icing onto the cookies with a pastry tube or spread it with a narrow, round-ended knife. Keep the icing covered with plastic wrap or aluminum foil when not in use.

Old-Fashioned Hot Cocoa

SERVES 8

1½ cups water
½ cup unsweetened cocoa powder
⅛ teaspoon salt
½ cup sugar
½ teaspon ground cinnamon
6 cups milk
1½ teaspoons vanilla extract
Candy canes
Marshmallows

1. Bring the water to a boil in a small heavy saucepan and remove from heat. Stir in the cocoa powder, salt, sugar, and cinnamon; then place over very low heat and simmer very gently just until the mixture has reached a slightly syrupy consistency, 2 to 3 minutes.

2. In a separate saucepan, heat the milk over low heat until just below the simmering point. Remove from heat and stir in the cocoa mixture. Stir in the vanilla, cover, and let stand for 5 minutes before serving.

3. Ladle the cocoa into mugs and garnish each with a candy cane or a marshmallow.

Making cocoa is so simple that there's really no need to use mixes that are filled with preservatives and artificial flavorings. The only "difficult" part of making cocoa is scalding the milk, and you have to do that with a mix, too, so why not make the real thing?

AN ANYTIME SUPPER

•

FOR 6 TO 8

MENU

Christmas Ribbon Slaw
Ken's Fish and Corn Chowder
Burlington Brown Bread
Cranberry–Nut Pudding

*C*hristmas Eve is usually hectic in most households—I know it often is in mine. This "anytime" supper allows time for last-minute chores, Christmas Eve vespers, or a ride around town to see all the holiday magic. Because everything's ready when needed, this supper can even be served as family members come and go or friends drop in—keep the chowder warming on top of the stove and the pudding warming in the oven. This is a night for the cook to relax—slow down, take it easy, and enjoy.

Getting Ready: The chowder can be made up to a day ahead, with the addition of the fish and the final simmering done just before serving, which takes only a few minutes. The coleslaw should be made a day, or even two, ahead, so the flavors can develop. The bread can also be made early in the day, or even a day ahead, but it shouldn't be made any earlier. The Cranberry–Nut Pudding, too, can be baked early in the day, or even the day

"He comes the brave old Christmas! His sturdy steps I hear; We will give him a hearty welcome, For he comes but once a year!"
Mary Howitt

before, and warmed up in a slow oven just before serving. Remember to have some vanilla ice cream in the freezer.

Beverages: I prefer cold cider or beer with this supper, but, if you'd like to have wine, try a California Chardonnay. With dessert I like a cup of hot, strong orange-spice tea. Have your homemade liqueurs handy, too.

Setting: There need be no special decorations here, since by now the whole house is probably festooned with Christmas garlands and ribbons. Set the table as casually as possible, and if you feel it looks a bit bare, add a few candles and make a pile of just-wrapped gifts in the center and let everyone wonder what's in them (Ho! Ho! Ho!).

Christmas Ribbon Slaw

SERVES 6 TO 8

2 cups shredded green cabbage
2 cups shredded red cabbage
2 carrots, peeled and grated
1 green pepper, seeded and grated
1 red pepper, seeded and grated
1 small red onion, peeled and grated
1 tart apple, cored and grated

Dressing
1 cup Homemade Mayonnaise (page 90)
¼ cup cider vinegar
1 tablespoon sugar
1 tablespoon Dijon mustard
1 teaspoon caraway or celery seeds
½ teaspoon salt
½ teaspoon freshly ground black pepper

1. Toss the vegetables and apple together in a large bowl.

2. In a separate bowl, or in the bowl of a food processor fitted with the steel chopping blade, combine the dressing ingredients and mix until smooth.

3. Pour the dressing over the vegetable mixture and toss. Cover and refrigerate for several hours, or preferably overnight. Toss again before serving.

There are probably as many recipes for coleslaw as there are heads of cabbage, but I like this version, which uses both red and green cabbage along with other colorful vegetables. This pretty combination makes a nice contrast to the creamy white chowder. Coleslaw is best when made a day or two ahead to allow the vegetables to marinate in the dressing.

Ken's Fish and Corn Chowder

SERVES 8

A hearty main-course soup, this chowder combines the flavors of the Northeast, Midwest, and, with an accent of hot green chili pepper, the Southwest. Use a food processor to chop the corn.

¼ pound lean salt pork, diced
¼ cup (½ stick) butter
2 medium onions, coarsely chopped
1 large green pepper, diced
2 garlic cloves, finely chopped
1 to 2 small green chili peppers, finely chopped
4 tablespoons all-purpose flour
3 cups fish stock *or* 2 cups clam juice and 1 cup water
3 cups (1½ pints) half-and-half
3 cups peeled and diced boiling potatoes
3 cups coarsely chopped corn
½ teaspoon dried thyme
2 pounds firm white fish fillets, such as cod or haddock
½ cup chopped parsley
Salt and freshly ground black pepper
Chopped parsley

1. Blanch the salt pork in boiling water for 5 minutes to remove excess saltiness. Drain and place in the bottom of a large heavy stockpot or Dutch oven. Add the butter, onions, green pepper, garlic, and green chili. Sauté over medium heat for 10 minutes, or until the onion becomes transparent.

2. Gradually add the flour, stirring to blend thoroughly. Slowly pour in the fish stock, stirring constantly; then stir in the half-and-half. Bring the mixture to a simmer; then add the potatoes, corn, and thyme. Simmer until the potatoes are not quite tender, 10 to 12 minutes. (The chowder may be prepared ahead to this point and refrigerated. Bring to a simmer again before proceeding.)

3. Cut the fish filets into 1-inch chunks; then add the fish and parsley to the pot. Simmer until the fish is just cooked through—opaque and easily flaked with a fork—about 5 minutes. Do not overcook. Taste and adjust the seasoning with salt and freshly ground black pepper.

4. Serve the chowder in large bowls, garnished with a sprinkling of chopped parsley and a twist of the pepper mill.

Burlington Brown Bread

MAKES ONE 8½ x 4½ x 3-INCH LOAF

This bread takes 2 hours to bake in a fairly slow oven, so you can stick it in and forget about it. Wrap presents or take a nap as the comforting aroma of freshly baked bread fills the house. This nutty and wheaty bread is good for breakfast, too, toasted and slathered with butter and honey or jam.

1 cup all-purpose flour
1 teaspoon salt
2½ teaspoons baking powder
1 teaspoon baking soda
2 cups whole wheat flour
¼ cup firmly packed dark brown sugar
¾ cup warm water
¾ cup milk
½ cup dark molasses
½ cup finely chopped walnuts
½ cup dark raisins

1. Preheat the oven to 275°F. Grease an 8½ × 4½ × 3-inch loaf pan.

2. In a medium mixing bowl, sift together the all-purpose flour, salt, baking powder, and baking soda. Add the whole wheat flour, and mix well.

3. In a separate large bowl, dissolve the brown sugar in the warm water; then stir in the milk and molasses. Stir the dry ingredients into this mixture until just blended; then fold in the nuts and raisins.

4. Pour the batter into the prepared pan and bake for 2 hours, or until the surface is well browned and a knife inserted in the center of the loaf comes out clean.

5. Remove the loaf from the pan and place it on its side on a wire rack to cool. Cooling for at least an hour before serving makes for easier slicing.

"Christmas won't be Christmas without any presents."
Little Women
Louisa May Alcott

Cranberry-Nut Pudding

SERVES 8

This fragrant pudding fills the house with the aromas of Christmas while it's baking. Here it's baked in one pan, but it's also nice made in individual ramekins or custard cups.

Filling
6 cups (2 12-ounce bags) cranberries
1 teaspoon grated orange rind
¼ cup orange juice
1 cup chopped pecans *or* walnuts
1 cup sugar
1 teaspoon ground cinnamon
½ teaspoon grated nutmeg
¼ cup (½ stick) butter, melted

Topping
1¾ cups sifted all-purpose flour
1 tablespoon sugar
1 tablespoon baking powder
½ teaspoon salt
½ teaspoon ground cinnamon
6 tablespoons cold butter
⅞ cup milk
2 tablespoons lightly beaten egg

1. Preheat the oven to 375°F. Butter a shallow round 2-quart baking dish or a 10-inch deep-dish pie pan, preferably ovenproof glass or earthenware.

2. Combine all filling ingredients and spread them in an even layer in the baking dish.

3. To make the topping, sift together the flour, sugar, baking powder, salt, and cinnamon. Cut in the butter with a pastry blender (or in the bowl of a food processor fitted with the steel chopping blade) until the mixture is the consistency of coarse cornmeal.

4. Pour in the milk and beat with a fork until the milk is just blended in, forming a stiff, sticky dough.

5. Drop the dough by tablespoonfuls onto the filling, leaving a few cracks for the cranberries to bubble up and steam to escape. Brush the surface of the dough with beaten egg and bake for 30 to 35 minutes, or until the top is golden brown.

6. Serve the pudding warm with a small scoop of vanilla ice cream or a dollop of sweetened whipped cream.

A FEAST OF SEVEN FISHES

•

FOR 8 TO 10

"...and then (sweetest of all) comes the quiet calmness of Christmas eve."

Christopher Morley

MENU

Crabmeat, Lobster, and Red Pepper Mousse
Cod Steaks with Lemon and Fennel
Cioppino della Casa with Spinach Fettuccine
Crusty Italian Bread
Lemon–Grapefruit Granita
Hazelnut Macaroons

*M*y friends of Italian extraction tell me that Christmas Eve has always overshadowed Christmas Day itself as the focus of celebration in Italian households. Christmas Eve day was traditionally a day of fasting, so the seafood dinner served after midnight mass was eagerly looked forward to. Why seven fishes? No one has been able to tell me, not even the most tradition-bound of my friends, but they do tell me that this feast is considered a source of good luck for the coming year.

This menu does have seven fishes and does have a strong Italian influence, but the individual dishes are not necessarily those traditionally served. I've pared down the traditional menu by combining fishes in the Cioppino della Casa, and introducing a very untraditional Crabmeat, Lobster, and Red Pepper Mousse. A light and refreshing granita follows the zesty cioppino.

Getting Ready: The granita and macaroons can be made up to several days in advance, and the mousse can be made up to a day ahead. Buy several loaves of crusty Italian or French bread when you do your marketing.

On Christmas Eve day, the cod steaks can be prepared up to the point at which they are put into the oven, then stored in the refrigerator. The sauce for the cioppino, too, can be made early in the day, or even the day before, and the shellfish can be cleaned several hours ahead.

About half an hour before serving, put on a pot of hot water for boiling the pasta and heat up the sauce for the cioppino if it was made in advance. About 20 minutes before serving, put the prepared cod steaks into the oven. Just before serving the cod, add the shellfish to the cioppino sauce to simmer, and cook the pasta. Just before serving the main course, remove the granita from the freezer to the refrigerator to soften a bit before serving.

Beverages: With the mousse and the cod steaks, try a well-chilled Frascati. I like to switch to a light red wine with the cioppino. Try a Valpolicella from Italy or a Gamay from California. After dessert, strong espresso served with Sambucca finishes the meal off nicely.

Setting: Set the table with a red-and-white-checked tablecloth (what else?), and lay a thick, lacy row of evergreen branches down the center, topped by artichokes, red peppers, and fat red candles. Tie red and green ribbons around white napkins and use plain white dishes, simple heavy flatware, and big simple wineglasses.

I like to play traditional Italian Christmas music during this feast as well as the popular Christmas standards sung by the likes of Sinatra, Como, and Pavarotti.

Menu Variations: You can mix and match the seafood used in each dish—just remember that they all have to total seven. For dessert, try to keep it light but flavorful after this strong-flavored meal—the Poached Pears in White Wine (page 221) would be good here.

Christmas Lights

●

Candles brighten spirits as well as rooms. When Perry Ellis was once asked what he would buy if he had but one hundred dollars to spend on furnishing a room, he said he would spend it all on candles, and his answer is especially appropriate during the holidays. Bring out every candle you've got stashed away: long, short, thick, thin; red, green, white, gold; pine, bayberry, citrus, cinnamon; and brighten your house and your spirits.

Originally, candles were burned at Christmas-time as companions to the Yule log and they were used to represent the divine light that shines over the world during the Christmas season. The candles we set in our windows are a tradition brought to America by the Irish; they lit their Yule candles in their windows to guide Mary and Joseph to their homes and to welcome them. Now we use candles as symbols of welcome, friendship, and joy.

Crabmeat, Lobster, and Red Pepper Mousse

SERVES 10

2 tablespoons unflavored gelatin
¾ cup cold water
1 cup boiling water
1 large roasted red pepper (page 90), coarsely chopped
1 medium red onion, coarsely chopped
1 cup Homemade Mayonnaise (page 90)
¼ teaspoon cayenne pepper
1 tablespoon lemon juice
1 cup heavy cream, whipped
1 cup cooked crabmeat, flaked
1 cup cooked lobster, flaked
Red lettuce leaves
Crackers *or* Melba Toasts (page 195)

1. Soften the gelatin in the cold water, then add the boiling water and stir well to dissolve. Chill until thick and syrupy, about 12 to 15 minutes.

2. Place the red pepper, red onion, mayonnaise, cayenne, and lemon juice in the bowl of a food processor fitted with the steel chopping blade, and process until smooth. Blend in the chilled gelatin.

3. In a separate large chilled bowl, whip the cream until stiff peaks form. Gently fold in the mixture from the processor and the crabmeat and lobster.

4. Gently transfer the mousse to a well-oiled 6-cup mold and chill until firm, at least 4 hours. To serve, unmold onto a platter and surround with red lettuce leaves. Serve with crackers or Melba Toast.

" 'Twas the night before Christmas, when all through the house
Not a creature was stirring, not even a mouse;
The stockings were hung by the chimney with care,
In hopes that St. Nicholas soon would be there."
Clement Clarke Moore
A Visit from St. Nicholas

Roasted Peppers

1. Preheat the broiler and place the peppers on a baking sheet. Broil as close to the heat source as possible until the skin is charred, turning occasionally to char all sides.

2. Or place the peppers on a long-handled fork, one at a time, over an open flame on top of the stove, turning to char evenly.

3. Sweat the peppers in a plastic bag for 5 minutes; then remove from the bag and pull off the charred skin with your fingers.

4. Cut the peppers open, seed them, and use as the recipe indicates.

Homemade Mayonnaise

MAKES ABOUT 2½ CUPS

Since I've had a food processor, I buy mayonnaise very infrequently. It takes but a few minutes to make and all the ingredients are generally on hand.

2 large egg yolks, at room temperature
1 whole large egg, at room temperature
1 teaspoon Dijon mustard
¼ cup red wine vinegar *or* lemon juice
1 cup olive oil
1 cup peanut *or* vegetable oil
Pinch of salt
Ground black *or* red pepper

1. Combine the yolks, whole egg, mustard, and vinegar or lemon juice in the bowl of a food processor fitted with a steel chopping blade. Process for 1 minute.

2. With the machine running, slowly add the oil through the tube in a thin, steady stream, almost a trickle.

3. After the oil is completely incorporated and the mayonnaise is thick and fluffy, season it with salt and pepper to taste. Add more lemon juice or blend in more oil, depending on the consistency desired.

4. Remove the mayonnaise to a jar, cover, and refrigerate. Mayonnaise will keep at least a week in the refrigerator.

Cod Steaks with Lemon and Fennel

SERVES 8 TO 10

Dried salt cod (baccalà) is a traditional fish for Christmas Eve, but I prefer the flavor and simplicity in preparation of fresh cod. Steaming the fish with lemon, fennel, and herbs keeps it moist and enhances its flavor.

2 medium onions, thinly sliced
2 whole garlic cloves
½ cup olive oil
2 tablespoons chopped parsley
½ teaspoon dried rosemary
½ teaspoon dried thyme
1 tablespoon fennel seeds, crushed
½ cup fresh lemon juice
8 to 10 cod steaks, about ⅜ inches thick
16 to 20 fennel stalks
8 to 10 thin lemon slices

1. Preheat the oven to 350°F.

2. In a small heavy saucepan, sauté the onions and garlic in the olive oil until tender, 10 to 15 minutes.

3. Stir in the herbs, fennel seeds, and lemon juice. Remove the garlic cloves and set the sauce aside.

4. Oil a shallow baking dish large enough to hold the fish in one layer; then arrange the fish and fennel stalks in it. Pour the sauce over the top of each steak and put a lemon slice over the sauce. Cover the baking dish tightly with aluminum foil. (The dish may be prepared ahead to this point, covered with aluminum foil, and stored in the refrigerator.)

5. Bake about 25 minutes, or until a cake tester inserted in the thickest part of the fish meets little resistance and comes out clean.

6. Serve each steak on a small plate garnished with two fennel stalks and a few grindings of black pepper.

Cioppino della Casa

SERVES 8 TO 10

Cioppino is one of California's greatest contributions to American cooking. When Italian immigrants settled in the San Francisco Bay area, they developed a Pacific version of their beloved Mediterranean seafood stews. This adaptation of cioppino—served untraditionally over pasta—is easy to prepare but requires a bit of careful timing and watching. Vary the shellfish to your own taste and local availability if you wish. Serve this with lots of good crusty bread to mop up the sauce left in the bottom of the plates.

2 tablespoons butter
6 tablespoons olive oil
2 medium onions, chopped
8 garlic cloves, chopped
1 large green pepper, coarsely chopped
3 cups canned Italian plum tomatoes
1 6-ounce can tomato paste
1 tablespoon dried thyme
12 whole black peppercorns, crushed
3 bay leaves
2 cups dry Italian red wine
24 to 30 jumbo shrimp, peeled and deveined
1 pound sea scallops
24 to 30 cherrystone clams, thoroughly scrubbed
24 to 30 mussels, debearded and thoroughly scrubbed
Salt and freshly ground black pepper to taste
2½ pounds fresh *or* 2 pounds dried spinach fettuccine

1. Place a very large pot of water on the stove and bring to a boil; then add 1 tablespoon salt.

2. On another burner, heat the butter and oil in a large Dutch oven or large heavy pot. Sauté the onions, garlic, and green pepper until tender, about 10 minutes. Stir in tomatoes, tomato paste, thyme, peppercorns, and bay leaves, and stir until smooth. Stir in wine and then simmer sauce, covered, over low heat for 45 minutes, stirring occasionally. (The sauce may be made ahead to this point and refrigerated. Reheat sauce before proceeding to step 3.)

3. Add the shellfish. Cover and simmer for 10 to 15 minutes, or until the clams and mussels have opened. Season the sauce with salt and pepper to taste. This dish should be quite peppery.

4. While the shellfish is cooking in the sauce, add the spinach fettuccine to the large pot of boiling salted water in step 1. If fresh, the pasta should take only 2 to 3 minutes to cook (dried pasta will take up to 10 minutes longer—check package directions).

5. Serve small mounds of pasta in individual bowls topped with an assortment of shellfish.

Lemon-Grapefruit Granita

SERVES 10

Refreshingly cool and light, this tart granita is a welcome relief to the palate at the end of a big and spicy meal.

2 cups sugar
2 cups water
Grated rind of 1 lemon
Grated rind of ½ grapefruit
3 cups fresh lemon juice
1 cup fresh grapefruit juice

Garnish
1 grapefruit, cut into sections
10 thin, round lemon slices
1 cup vodka
10 mint sprigs

1. Combine the sugar and water in a saucepan and bring to a boil. Simmer for 5 minutes. Stir in the grated rinds, remove from heat, and cool to room temperature.

2. Add the juices to the syrup mixture. If using an ice-cream maker, follow the manufacturer's instructions, *or* freeze as follows.

3. Pour the mixture into a shallow metal pan and place in the freezer. Freeze for 4 hours, breaking up the layers of ice with a fork that form every hour.

4. For garnish, place the grapefruit sections, lemon slices, and vodka in a small bowl, cover and place in the freezer until serving time (vodka will chill but will not solidify).

5. Remove the granita from the freezer and cut the ice into pieces. Place the pieces in a blender or the bowl of a food processor fitted with a metal chopping blade. Blend at low speed or process slowly using short pulses until the mixture becomes slightly grainy. Stop blending before the mixture begins to liquefy.

6. Serve immediately, or return to the pan in the freezer and then allow to soften slightly before serving. To serve, spoon the granita into stemmed glasses. Garnish each serving with one grapefruit section, one lemon slice, and a mint sprig. Splash a bit of the chilled, flavored vodka over each serving.

Hazelnut Macaroons

MAKES ABOUT 5 DOZEN COOKIES

These light and delicate morsels can be stored for several weeks in a tightly covered container in a cool place.

1½ cups finely chopped hazelnuts
5 large egg whites
½ teaspoon salt
¼ teaspoon cream of tartar
2 tablespoons Frangelico liqueur
1⅓ cups sugar
1 cup shredded coconut

1. Preheat the oven to 325°F. Grease two baking sheets well.

2. On a separate ungreased baking sheet spread the hazelnuts in a thin layer. Place in the oven and toast for 10 to 12 minutes, or until lightly browned. Remove from the oven and set aside.

3. In a large mixing bowl, beat the egg whites until they form soft peaks. Gradually beat in the salt and cream of tartar, then the liqueur, 1 teaspoonful at a time. Continue beating until the whites regain their peaks.

4. Gradually beat in the sugar, beating continuously until the mixture is stiff but not dry. Gently fold in the coconut and hazelnuts.

5. Drop the dough by teaspoonfuls onto the prepared baking sheets about 1½ inches apart. Bake for 20 to 25 minutes, or until the edges are lightly browned. When done, remove to a wire rack to cool.

CITY-MORNING BRUNCH

•

FOR 6

MENU

Cranberry Mimosas

Iva Mae's Holiday Stollen

Bacon–Vegetable Hash

Herbed Baked Eggs in Tomatoes

Clara's Apple Dumplings with Cream

"Small cheer and great welcome makes a merry feast."
Shakespeare

On the farm, breakfast was always very, very early. When I came to the city, I discovered a much lazier version of breakfast, brunch, which is really just a late breakfast with a drink (or is it an early lunch with a drink?). So here's a lazier way to spend Christmas morning, whether you live in a city high rise or an old farmhouse.

Get everyone started with Cranberry Mimosas, a platter of sliced stollen, and a pot of hot coffee, while the cook goes to work. As a matter of fact, why not join them and start the cooking a bit later?

Getting Ready: This menu really doesn't require much work just before serving. The stollen takes quite a bit of time, but it should be made a day or two ahead, anyway; or it can be made well in advance and frozen, tightly wrapped.

If the pastry crust for the apple dumplings has been made ahead and chilled, that takes away some of the last-minute bother, too. The crust can be rolled out, filled, and put in the oven about an hour and a half before you want to serve the dumplings.

Scoop out the tomatoes for the baked eggs and take the eggs out of the refrigerator to come to room temperature about an hour before serving. Next start cooking the hash (you might even chop the bacon and vegetables the night before and store them in the refrigerator). It will keep well over low heat if the tomatoes aren't quite done when it is. Sauté the shallots and fill the tomato shells next. Put them in the oven about half an hour before serving. Time yourself so they go into the oven just as the apple dumplings come out—this will give the dumplings time to cool off a little before you serve them.

Beverages: A pot of hot coffee is a must, but instead of the Cranberry Mimosas, you might want to serve traditional Mimosas (Champagne and orange juice), Cape Codders (vodka and cranberry juice cocktail on the rocks), or Sea Breezes (Cape Codders with a splash of grapefruit juice). I wouldn't recommend Bloody Marys here, as they compete with the eggs. Of course, for those who don't want alcohol with brunch, fresh orange juice, grapefruit juice, or cranberry juice cocktail would go well, too.

Setting: We're being lazy here, so set the table simply. I like to use red and green tartan plaid place mats and napkins with small tin cookie cutters for napkin rings, and use plain earthenware dishes. In the center of the table I place a small potted poinsettia or Christmas cactus, borrowed from somewhere else in the house, or a bowl of fresh fruit.

Cranberry Mimosas

These pretty, sparkling eye-openers couldn't be easier to make. Don't limit these to the holiday season—they're equally refreshing when the sun is setting slowly in the summer sky.

Fresh cranberries
Chilled Champagne
Chilled cranberry juice cocktail

Place 3 fresh cranberries into each glass (use Champagne flutes, or tall, stemmed wineglasses). Fill the glasses about half full with Champagne; then fill to the two-thirds point with the cranberry juice cocktail. Serve at once.

Iva Mae's Holiday Stollen

A traditional German fruit bread, stollen has become an American standard as well at Christmastime. This recipe comes from one of the best bakers I know, who got it from a neighbor who was a native of Germany. Make the stollen a day or two in advance to allow the flavor and texture to mellow, and store it at room temperature, tightly wrapped. Stollen keeps well in the freezer—in fact, Iva Mae saves one of her Christmas loaves to serve for breakfast on the Fourth of July!

¾ cup milk
½ cup sugar
½ teaspoon salt
2 packets active dry yeast
½ cup lukewarm water
1 cup all-purpose flour
2 large eggs, lightly beaten
¾ cup (1½ sticks) butter, softened
4 to 5 cups sifted all-purpose flour
¼ teaspoon grated nutmeg
1½ cups dried currants
½ cup chopped candied citron
½ cup chopped candied lemon peel
½ cup chopped candied cherries
Grated lemon rind of 1 lemon
½ cup coarsely chopped almonds
½ cup (1 stick) butter, melted
Confectioners' sugar

1. Scald the milk over medium heat; then stir in the sugar and salt. Remove from heat and cool to room temperature.

2. In a large mixing bowl, dissolve the yeast in the lukewarm water; then stir in the 1 cup flour. Gradually pour in the scalded milk mixture; then mix until blended. Cover the bowl with a clean dish towel and let dough rise in a warm place until doubled in bulk.

3. When the sponge has risen, add the eggs, softened butter, 4 cups flour, and the nutmeg, and mix well. Fold in the currants, chopped candied fruits, grated lemon rind, and nuts.

4. Remove the dough to a floured board and knead until the dough is very elastic. Add a bit of flour, if necessary, to keep the dough from sticking.

5. Remove the dough to a buttered mixing bowl and brush the surface with some of the melted butter. Cover the bowl with the towel and let the dough rise again until doubled in bulk.

6. Punch down the dough and divide it into two equal portions. Roll each half into a rounded rectangle about ½ inch thick, and brush the surface with the remaining melted butter. Fold the dough

The Wreath on the Front Door

•

The Christmas wreath, with its ring shape symbolizing eternal peace and joy, expresses these good wishes to everyone who walks through or past your door during the Yuletide season. Your local greenhouse, florist, craft shop, or even the five-and-dime has all the materials you need to make your own wreath. Here are a few suggestions:

A pine cone wreath with clusters of nuts and a plaid bow.

A wreath made of artemisia, statice, baby's breath, and other dried flowers.

An evergreen wreath with small lace fans, baby's breath, and bows of narrow pink and purple ribbon.

A grapevine wreath studded with dried red and green chili peppers.

Clusters of nuts, oranges, lady apples, and red berries on boxwood and evergreen.

Branches of eucalyptus formed into a wreath and wrapped up with red and white ribbons.

A holly wreath with tiny silver balls and a big silver bow.

A wreath of magnolia leaves studded with apples and decorated with a red-and-green plaid bow.

over lengthwise, not quite in half, and place on a lightly greased baking sheet. Cover the loaves with the towel and let rise again until doubled in bulk.

7. Preheat the oven to 350°F. Bake the loaves about 50 minutes, or until they are nicely browned. Remove the loaves to wire racks and cool to room temperature. Just before serving, dust with confectioners' sugar. Serve sliced with soft butter.

Bacon-Vegetable Hash

SERVES 6 TO 8

½ pound lean slab bacon, diced
3 tablespoons butter
6 medium russet potatoes, unpeeled and diced
1 large green pepper, diced
1 medium onion, coarsely chopped
½ pound mushrooms, coarsely chopped
Salt
Freshly ground black pepper

1. Place the diced bacon in a large cold skillet and sauté over low heat. When evenly browned, and the fat is rendered, drain the bacon on paper towels and set it aside. Pour off all but 3 tablespoons of the bacon drippings and discard.

2. Melt the butter in the pan with the remaining bacon drippings. Add the potatoes, green pepper, onion, and mushrooms. Sauté over medium heat until the potatoes are tender, about 20 minutes, stirring frequently. Add a bit more butter, if necessary, to prevent sticking.

3. Add the reserved bacon, salt to taste, and plenty of fresh black pepper. Sauté for an additional 5 minutes to allow flavors to blend. Serve warm.

Vegetarian Hash Omit the bacon and substitute 2 tablespoons olive oil. Increase the butter to 4 tablespoons.

Herbed Baked Eggs in Tomatoes

SERVES 6

---

6 medium ripe tomatoes
2 tablespoons butter
3 small shallots, finely chopped
4 tablespoons finely chopped parsley
½ teaspoon dried chervil
½ teaspoon dried tarragon
Salt and freshly ground black pepper
¾ cup grated Swiss *or* Gruyère cheese
6 extra large eggs, at room temperature
¼ cup fine dry bread crumbs
2 tablespoons butter, melted
Parsley sprigs

1. Preheat the oven to 400°F.

2. Cut off the stem end of each tomato and scoop out the seeds and most of the pulp with a teaspoon. Turn the tomatoes upside down on paper towels to drain.

3. Melt 2 tablespoons butter in a small skillet over medium heat. Add the shallots and sauté until soft, about 5 minutes. Stir in 3 tablespoons of the parsley and the chervil and tarragon.

4. Stand the tomatoes right side up in an oiled shallow baking dish just large enough to hold them and season the insides with salt and pepper. Then divide the shallot-herb mixture among them, coating the inside of each tomato. Sprinkle 1 tablespoon grated cheese into each.

5. Carefully break 1 egg into each tomato and sprinkle the tops with the remaining cheese. Combine the bread crumbs with the remaining chopped parsley and sprinkle over the cheese; then drizzle melted butter over all.

6. Place in the oven and bake until the eggs are set, 30 to 35 minutes. Serve warm, garnished with parsley sprigs.

Clara's Apple Dumplings

MAKES 6

Of all the dishes my mother makes, this is my favorite. When I was little, she always told me that our apple trees were planted by Johnny Appleseed, who lived for a time in nearby Mansfield. Years later I found out that just about everyone who grew up in northern Ohio heard the same story! Mom serves these warm with sweet cream or vanilla ice cream.

A NOUVELLE NOEL DINNER, where traditional and new flavors meet on Christmas Day, is a colorful new classic dramatically set against an all-white background. The main course consists of Grilled Pork Medallions with Pear and Tangerine Chutney; Sautéed Sweet Potatoes Julienne; Snow Peas in Black Butter; and Red and Green Pepper Salad.

1 recipe Pastry Crust (page 47)
6 medium Granny Smith *or* other tart baking apples
Light brown sugar
Ground cinnamon
Grated nutmeg
Butter
Milk
Granulated sugar

1. Preheat the oven to 375°F. Roll out the pastry dough to a rectangle about 10 × 15 inches. Cut the dough with a sharp floured knife into six 5-inch squares.

2. Peel and slice the apples, and divide them into mounds on the center of each dough square. Sprinkle each with about 2 teaspoons brown sugar, a generous sprinkling of cinnamon, and a pinch or two of nutmeg. Dot with butter.

3. Moisten the edges of pastry with milk. Fold the corners and sides of pastry up over the center of the apples and pinch all edges together to seal. Don't try to make this too neat—the dumplings should look rather rustic.

4. Transfer the dumplings to a greased shallow baking pan and brush the top of each with milk and sprinkle each with a small amount of sugar. Prick with a fork to allow steam to escape during baking. Bake for about 40 minutes, or until the pastry is nicely browned. Serve warm.

AN ALL-AMERICAN OPEN HOUSE BUFFET DINNER for Christmas Day gives equal billing to some of my favorite Santa Clauses from my collection and to this new traditional menu (counter-clockwise from center): Twin Turkey Roulades; Marinated Broccoli Salad; Old-Fashioned Fresh Cranberry Relish; Purees of Yellow and White Winter Vegetables; Pumpkin-Praline Cheesecake; Steamed Ginger Pudding; and Cranberry Fool.

A PLANTATION DINNER on Christmas Day features a pineapple and fruit centerpiece on a bed of evergreens and magnolia leaves, a sign of Southern hospitality and gracious living. The main course awaits on the sideboard (from the left): Roasted Capon stuffed with Corn Bread Pudding; Green Beans with Salt Pork; Glazed Country Ham with Brandied Peaches; and Bourbon-Laced Sweet Potato Puree.

102

COUNTRY-MORNING BREAKFAST

•

FOR 6

COUNTRY-MORNING BREAKFAST—they'll be home for Christmas! Here's heartwarming fare for a cold Christmas morning: Scrambled Eggs with Chives, Dill, and Red Peppers; Homemade Sausage Patties with Sautéed Pears; and Hot Popovers with Quick Homemade Jam.

MENU
Hot Popovers
Fresh Sausage Patties with Sautéed Pears
Scrambled Eggs with Chives, Dill, and Red Peppers
Quick Homemade Jam

*R*emember the Christmas mornings of your childhood, when you weren't allowed to go downstairs until your parents woke up? Well, if the anticipation of gifts under the tree and filled stockings hanging at the mantel doesn't get everybody up early on Christmas morning, the aromas of this hearty breakfast—fresh sausage sautéing, popovers baking, and jam simmering—certainly will. If only every morning could be Christmas!

Getting Ready: This entire menu can be prepared in about an hour. Both the sausage patties and the jam can be made ahead, but they're so quick and easy that it's hardly necessary.

First, pare the fruit for the jam and the pears. The jam can simmer on the stove while the oven is heating for the popovers and the batter is being mixed.

While the popovers are baking, make the sausage, shape into patties, and start sautéing them. Keeping an eye on the jam and sausage patties, start sautéing the pears. Then chop the pepper and dill for the eggs, and sauté the pepper. The jam should be ready at this point.

About 10 minutes before the popovers are ready to come out of the oven, scramble the eggs and begin cooking. Everything should be ready to serve at about the same time.

Beverages: A big pot of coffee should go on the stove before you start cooking—for the cook and the early risers, and to serve with breakfast. And, of course, a big pitcher of freshly squeezed orange juice. If you're serving this menu as a brunch, you might also want to add Samantha's Fabulous Bloodies (page 213) or Cranberry Mimosas (page 96).

Setting: This should be pretty much of a no-fuss affair, but it's nice to fill a basket or antique wooden bowl with evergreens and pine cones for the center of the table. Put a small, wrapped "stocking stuffer" gift at each place to get the day off to a festive start.

Hot Popovers

MAKES 12 POPOVERS

3 large eggs
1½ cups milk
1½ cups sifted all-purpose flour
1½ tablespoons butter, melted
¼ teaspoon salt

1. Preheat the oven to 450°F. Grease a popover pan or heavy, deep muffin pan well, and place in the oven. (Do not use thin aluminum pans—if you don't have a popover pan or heavy muffin tin, use custard cups set on a baking sheet.)

2. In a mixing bowl, preferably one with a pouring spout, beat the eggs thoroughly; then beat in the milk. Beat in the other ingredients until the batter is just smooth; do not overmix.

3. Remove the hot pan from the oven and immediately pour the batter into the cups until they are about two-thirds full. Return the pan to the oven and bake for 20 minutes.

4. Lower the oven temperature to 350°F., but *do not open the oven.* Bake for an additional 15 to 20 minutes, or until the popovers are firm and golden brown. (It's okay to open the oven to check for doneness after 30 minutes total baking time.) Serve the popovers hot with butter and Quick Homemade Jam.

Quick Homemade Jam
•

This method works well with strawberries, cranberries, apples, pears, and other firm fruit.

Combine 1 cup peeled and chopped fruit, 1 tablespoon water, and 1 tablespoon lemon juice in a small heavy saucepan. Bring to a simmer over medium heat; then slowly add ¾ cup sugar, stirring constantly until dissolved. Continue cooking until the fruit is very tender and the jam has thickened. Stir frequently, crushing the fruit against the side of the saucepan. Serve warm.

On a recent trip to Maine, I was reintroduced to this childhood favorite at the Jordan Pond House in Acadia National Park, where they are served piping hot at teatime with butter and delicious preserves.

Fresh Sausage Patties

2 pounds lean pork *or* 1 pound lean pork and 1 pound lean veal
1 pound pork fat
1½ teaspoons salt
1 teaspoon dried sage
½ teaspoon dried thyme
¼ teaspoon cayenne pepper
¼ teaspoon freshly ground black pepper

1. Cut the meat and fat into rough 1-inch cubes, and place them in the bowl of a food processor fitted with the metal chopping blade. Process until finely chopped. Add the seasonings and process just until well blended.

2. Remove the sausage mixture from the processor and divide it into fourths. Divide each section into thirds and shape into ½-inch-thick patties.

3. Place the patties in a large skillet over moderate heat. Sauté until well done and evenly browned on both sides, 15 to 20 minutes, pouring off fat as it accumulates in the pan. Serve on a warmed platter surrounded by Sautéed Pears.

Sautéed Pears

SERVES 6

3 tablespoons butter
6 firm ripe pears
2 tablespoons light brown sugar
¼ teaspoon ground cinnamon
¼ teaspoon ground ginger

1. Melt the butter in a large skillet over low heat. Meanwhile, peel and core the pears and cut them into ¼-inch slices.

2. Add the pear slices to the skillet and sauté gently until tender, but still firm, 5 to 7 minutes. Sprinkle the brown sugar and spices over the pears and toss. Sauté the mixture another minute or so, until the pears are glazed. Serve warm with Fresh Sausage Patties.

We've become so accustomed to using packaged sausage from the supermarket that we've forgotten how delicious homemade, additive-free country sausage can be. With the food processor, sausage-making is a simple task that takes only a few minutes. Sausage patties can be made ahead and frozen, well wrapped.

Scrambled Eggs with Chives, Dill, and Red Peppers

SERVES 6

Bright flecks of red and green add both a visual and flavorful spark to buttery scrambled eggs.

½ cup (1 stick) butter
1 large red pepper, chopped
12 extra-large eggs
½ teaspoon salt
¼ teaspoon cayenne pepper, or to taste
2 tablespoons snipped chives
3 tablespoons chopped fresh dill
Dill sprigs

1. In a large skillet over low heat melt the butter. Gently sauté the red pepper until crisp-tender, about 10 minutes.

2. Beat the eggs, salt, cayenne pepper, chives, and dill together with a fork. Raise the heat to medium-high and allow the skillet to heat up. The pan is ready when a few drops of water sprinkled into it sizzle gently.

3. Add the egg mixture to the skillet. When the eggs begin to set, begin stirring with a spatula, gently allowing the uncooked mixture to reach the surface of the skillet. Continue cooking until the eggs have reached not quite the desired doneness (the eggs will continue to cook a bit from their own heat). Immediately remove to a warm serving dish, garnished with sprigs of fresh dill.

A PLANTATION DINNER

•

FOR 10 TO 12

MENU

Oysters with Scarlett Sauce

Glazed Country Ham with Brandied Peaches (page 21)
and Hot Honey Mustard (page 24)

Roasted Capon Stuffed with Corn Bread Pudding

Green Beans with Salt Pork

Creamed Onions with Peanuts

Bourbon-Laced Sweet Potato Puree

"Barnes's Best" Eggnog

Martha Washington's White Fruitcake (page 20)

Lindsay Miller's Bourbon Balls (page 15)

"The extreame winde, rayne, froste and snow caused us to keepe *Christmas* among the savages where we were never more merry, nor fed on more plenty of good Oysters, Fish, Flesh, Wilde Fowl and good bread, nor never had better fires in England."
A Found Diary
Virginia,
December 25, 1613

Southern cuisine is one of my favorites: it has no fussiness or pretentions, yet it is elegant and delectable. This menu, based on Deep South tradition, is served every Christmas at our house, even though we're Yankees.

This is a big, big dinner. We usually take a break between the main course and dessert, which gives us time to let everything sink in before indulging again. There will probably be some ham left over, but that's only a bonus. Bake a batch of biscuits the next day and serve them split with slivers of ham and a good chutney. I've also included a recipe for a lentil soup that makes good use of the ham bone.

Getting Ready: Aside from the food itself, the best part of this menu is that a great deal of the preparation can be taken care of ahead of time. I usually do a lot of the work on Christmas Eve day at a leisurely pace.

If you're cooking the ham from scratch, and I recommend you do, the first thing to do is soak the ham—do this on the night of December 23. The ham has to soak overnight, and can be simmered and skinned the next day.

The Bourbon Balls and White Fruitcake are already in the larder (see pages 15 and 20). So are the Brandied Peaches (see page 21) but if you didn't make them yourself, good-quality brandied peaches are available at many gourmet shops.

The Scarlett Sauce for the oysters, Bourbon-Laced Sweet Potatoes, Creamed Onions with Peanuts, and Peach Glaze can all be made a day ahead; the sweet potatoes and onions need only be heated up in the oven just before serving. The eggnog can also be begun a day ahead.

The Corn Bread Pudding can be prepared early on Christmas Day. Do not stuff the capon, however, until you're ready to roast it. The capon, once stuffed, roasts with little watching on Christmas Day, as does the ham. The Green Beans with Salt Pork take very little time—start them about half an hour before dinner.

The last thing to do before sitting down is opening the oysters, which should be done immediately before serving with the help of a volunteer.

To complete the eggnog, whip the cream and egg whites and fold everything together after the main course.

Beverages: Eggnog is a Southern specialty, but I find it far too heavy and sweet to serve *before* a big dinner. Here it serves as dessert. Make a batch without liquor for the teetotalers and children. Serve a dry California Grenache Rosé as an aperitif before sitting down at the table. The oysters are best served without wine, as the sauce is tart. With the main course, continue with the rosé (I ordinarily find most rosés too sweet with dinner, but it goes nicely with this menu). Serve strong coffee afterward and maybe a bit of good old-fashioned Southern Comfort.

Setting: For this dinner, our dining table is always fully extended, which affords the opportunity for an elaborate centerpiece. In the middle of the table stands a pineapple, the traditional Southern and Colonial sign of welcome, surrounded by shiny red apples and bright lemons and limes. All of these fruits are nestled on a bed of magnolia leaves, holly, and wisps of evergreen branches,

"He was a bold man that first ate an oyster."

Dean Swift

Oyster Shucking

•

Scrub the oyster shells with a stiff brush under cold running water. Insert the end of an oyster knife or other strong, small sharp knife between the shells near the hinge. Holding the oyster over a bowl to catch the oyster liquor, twist the shell halves to open and cut the muscle with the knife. Then cut the oyster muscle from the other half of the shell.

A perfect complement to fresh oysters, this sauce is certainly worthy of its namesake: it's fiery, tangy, and irresistible. The sauce should be made a day in advance.

which runs down the center of the table. Crystal candlesticks with snowy white candles are evenly spaced along the bed of greens. This colorful table decoration looks spectacular on a white damask tablecloth, set with red-and-gold-bordered china on gleaming brass service plates, sparkling crystal, and gold-plated flatware.

Menu Variations: In our house, there is never any variation in this menu, because someone would be disappointed if a favorite dish was left out. However, if you don't want to bother with two meats, eliminate the capon and bake the Corn Bread Pudding in a casserole. For dessert you might also try the Chocolate Pecan Pie on page 160 rather than the White Fruit Cake, Bourbon Balls, and Eggnog; it's an honest-to-goodness Southern recipe direct from Winston-Salem, North Carolina. Or try the Lime Chess Tartlets on page 158. If you feel you want to serve an hors d'oeuvre before dinner, the Red Pepper Cheese on page 194 is an old Southern favorite. I prefer to pass only a small bowl of nuts with the before-dinner drinks.

Oysters with Scarlett Sauce

SERVES 12

1½ cups red wine vinegar
4 tablespoons finely chopped shallots
2 tablespoons freshly grated horseradish
¼ cup minced parsley
¾ teaspoon cracked black pepper
¼ teaspoon cayenne pepepr
4 dozen oysters
Parsley
Lemon wedges

1. To make the sauce, combine all the ingredients except the oysters in a tightly covered container and shake. Refrigerate for 24 hours, shaking occasionally.

2. Just before serving, shuck the oysters, leaving them on the half shell. Place a small bowl in the center of each of twelve salad plates and fill with the sauce; then surround each bowl with 4 oysters. Serve at once, garnished with parsley and lemon wedges.

Glazed Country Ham

SERVES 12, WITH LEFTOVERS

A homecooked, cured country ham is a gourmet tradition of the South, and a far cry from the precooked boiled hams found in most supermarket meat cases. Smithfield hams from Virginia are dry-cured, smoked, and gently aged to achieve their rich flavor. Remember that the ham needs to soak overnight before cooking, so plan accordingly.

1 country ham, 12 to 14 pounds
Peach Glaze (recipe follows)
Brandied Peaches (page 21)

1. Using a stiff brush, scrub the ham to remove the pepper coating and mold. Place the ham in a large pot with enough cold water to cover. Cover the pot and soak overnight at room temperature.

2. Drain the ham well and rinse; then return it to the pot and cover with cold water again. Place on the stove and bring the water to a simmer. Simmer, loosely covered, for 20 minutes per pound, or until the ham reaches an internal temperature of 150°F. Add water as needed to keep the ham covered during cooking.

3. When the ham is cooked, remove it from the water and allow to cool enough to handle easily. With a sharp knife, remove the tough rind, and carve away almost all of the outer fat, leaving only a ⅛-inch layer. Ham can be prepared ahead up to this point. When fully cool, wrap the ham in foil or plastic wrap and refrigerate.

4. About 2 hours before serving, preheat the oven to 350°F. Remove the ham from the refrigerator, unwrap, and place on a rack in a shallow roasting pan, flatter side down. Diagonally score the layer of fat, being careful not to cut into the meat itself; then spread a thin layer of Peach Glaze over the surface. Bake the ham for about 15 minutes per pound, brushing with glaze as needed.

5. Serve the ham on a platter surrounded by Brandied Peaches. Carve into very thin slices, as this ham is quite rich.

Peach Glaze
1 cup good-quality peach jam
¼ cup packed light brown sugar
¼ cup peach or apricot brandy
1 teaspoon dry mustard

1. Place all the ingredients in a small saucepan over medium-high heat. Stirring constantly, bring the mixture to a simmer; then continue cooking until it reaches a thick, syrupy consistency.

2. Remove from heat, cool, and refrigerate.

Roasted Capon Stuffed with Corn Bread Pudding

SERVES 10 TO 12

Capons, neutered male chickens, have tender flesh and a generous fat layer under the skin, yielding a very moist bird. I ate my first capon in Charleston, so this bird will always seem Southern to me.

1 oven-ready capon, about 8 pounds
Salt and freshly ground black pepper
Corn Bread Pudding (recipe follows)

1. Preheat the oven to 350°F. Wash the capon inside and out and dry with paper towels. Season the body and cavities with salt and pepper.

2. Stuff the bird loosely with Corn Bread Pudding and close the openings at either end with trussing skewers and string. Extra stuffing can be baked separately in a buttered baking dish.

3. Place the capon, breast up, on a rack in a roasting pan. Roast for 30 minutes per pound, or until the juices run clear when the drumstick is pierced with a fork. Baste frequently with the pan juices while roasting.

4. Remove the capon from the oven 15 minutes before serving and allow to rest, loosely covered, before carving.

5. Serve on a warm platter surrounded by holly leaves.

Corn Bread Pudding

SERVES 10 TO 12

Make your own corn bread, without sugar, as real Southerners do. It can be made ahead and frozen until needed.

3 medium onions, chopped
½ cup chopped parsley
5 medium celery stalks, chopped
1 medium green pepper, chopped
½ cup (1 stick) butter
4 cups coarse corn bread crumbs
3 cups cream-style corn
4 eggs, beaten
½ teaspoon dried thyme
½ teaspoon rubbed sage
Salt and freshly ground black pepper

1. In a heavy skillet, sauté the onions, parsley, celery, and green pepper in butter until the onions become transparent. Meanwhile, spread the corn bread crumbs on an aluminum foil–covered baking sheet and toast very lightly in a 325°F. oven for about 10 minutes.

2. In a mixing bowl, lightly mix all the ingredients. Season with salt and pepper to taste.

3. The pudding is now ready to use as stuffing. If, however, you're serving this without capon, place the mixture in a well-buttered 2-quart baking dish and bake at 350°F. for about 40 minutes, or until the surface is nicely browned.

Green Beans with Salt Pork

SERVES 10 to 12

2 pounds green beans, trimmed and washed
¼ pound lean salt pork

1. Cut the rind from the salt pork and rinse to remove excess surface salt. In a small saucepan, blanch the pork for 10 minutes.

2. Place the green beans in a large saucepan, cover with water and cook until just tender (boiling is better than steaming for this dish).

3. While the beans are cooking, cut the salt pork into ¼-inch cubes and place in a skillet and sauté for 10 minutes to render the fat. Pour off all but 3 tablespoons of fat.

4. Drain the beans and return them to the warm pot. Pour the salt pork and fat over the beans and toss. (May be made ahead up to this point, covered, and refrigerated. Warm slowly in a skillet over low heat.) Remove from the pot with a slotted spoon to drain off the excess fat and serve in a warmed vegetable dish.

5. Sauté 5 minutes over low heat, tossing occasionally.

"Christmas in the Air"

•

One of the most delightful aspects of the holiday season is the mélange of wonderful smells that can be found wafting into every room of the house. Try some of these ideas to make your home smell of the season:

Mix sliced orange peel, sliced apples, and cloves in a shallow bowl and set it out to perfume the air.

Set out bowls of spicy potpourri, and toss the mixture now and then to allow the air and scents to circulate

If you have an artificial Christmas tree (shame!) make beribboned arrangements of fresh evergreen boughs, or drape evergreen across the mantel or down a banister.

Dab pine oil onto unlit light bulbs; when they're turned on, their low heat will spread the scent.

When you want a nice citrusy scent in the kitchen, toss rinds into a pot with some whole cloves, whole allspice, and a cinnamon stick. Cover with water and simmer away.

Stud a whole orange all over with cloves, insert a hook, and hang it on the Christmas tree.

If you have a fireplace, toss a few cinnamon sticks or fresh pine branches onto the fire.

Use scented candles: bayberry, pine, or spice.

Creamed Onions with Peanuts

SERVES 10 TO 12

This recipe is adapted from one served in Colonial Williamsburg, Virginia. The peanuts add subtle flavor and crunch to what would otherwise be a rather bland dish.

30 small yellow *or* white onions, peeled
4 scallions, finely chopped
2 tablespoons butter
2 tablespoons all-purpose flour
2 cups milk
¼ cup chunky peanut butter
⅔ cup coarsely chopped salted peanuts (not dry-roasted)
Salt and freshly ground black pepper
½ cup buttered bread crumbs

1. Place the onions in a large saucepan with enough water to cover; then place on the stove and boil until just tender, about 15 minutes (do not overcook). Drain.

2. While the onions are cooking, sauté the scallions in butter, in a heavy medium saucepan, until tender. Stir in the flour. Slowly add the milk and simmer gently, stirring until smooth and slightly thickened. Add the peanut butter and stir until blended; then stir in ⅓ cup peanuts. Season the sauce with salt and pepper to taste.

3. Transfer the onions to a buttered 2-quart flat baking dish, and pour the sauce over them. Top with buttered bread crumbs and the remaining ⅓ cup chopped peanuts. This dish may be made ahead up to this point. Let cool and cover with aluminum foil or plastic wrap and refrigerate.

4. Two hours before serving, remove the dish from the refrigerator to allow it to come to room temperature. When the ham and capon come out of the oven, raise the oven temperature to 400°F. Place the creamed onions in the oven and bake for 15 minutes, or until the sauce begins to bubble and surface is lightly browned.

**"This is every cook's opinion:
No savory dish without an onion.
But lest your kissing should be spoiled,
Your onion must be thoroughly boiled."**
Dean Swift

Bourbon-Laced Sweet Potato Puree

SERVES 10 TO 12

3 pounds sweet potatoes
¼ cup (½ stick) butter
¼ cup packed dark brown sugar
1 teaspoon salt
¾ teaspoon ground cinnamon
½ teaspoon grated nutmeg
½ cup milk
½ cup bourbon

1. Place the unpeeled sweet potatoes in a large saucepan with enough water to cover and boil until tender, 20 to 25 minutes. When done, remove from the pan and peel while still warm.

2. Place the peeled sweet potatoes in a mixing bowl and mash by hand with a potato masher (do *not* use a food processor). Add the butter and dry ingredients and mash until smooth; then blend in the milk and bourbon, making a smooth, moist puree.

3. Transfer to a buttered 2-quart baking dish. Dot the surface with butter and sprinkle lightly with additional brown sugar. (This may be prepared ahead up to this point. Allow to cool; then cover and refrigerate.)

4. Remove from the refrigerator and preheat the oven to 350°F. Bake for about 45 minutes, or until the surface is lightly browned.

Note: If you're not preparing this dish ahead, it can be served at the end of step 2 in a warmed vegetable dish.

"The true essentials of a feast are only fun and feed."
Oliver Wendell Holmes

"Barnes's Best" Eggnog

SERVES 10, WITH SECONDS

¾ cup sugar
12 large eggs, separated
½ teaspoon salt
1 quart milk
1 cup heavy cream
½ cup brandy
½ cup light rum
Freshly grated nutmeg

1. Blend ½ cup sugar, the egg yolks, and salt together in the top of a double boiler over simmering water. Gradually stir in the milk and cook, stirring constantly, until the mixture is thick enough to coat the back of a spoon. Remove from the heat, cool, cover, and chill. May be prepared in advance up to this point.

2. Beat the egg whites until stiff peaks form; then beat in the remaining ¼ cup sugar. In a separate chilled bowl, whip the cream until stiff peaks form.

3. Pour the chilled mixture into a large punch bowl; then stir in the brandy and rum. Fold in the egg whites and then the whipped cream.

4. Ladle into punch glasses and dust each serving with grated nutmeg.

Teetotaler's Eggnog Omit the brandy and rum, and substitute 1 cup milk and 1 teaspoon rum extract.

"A Goodly Drink of Eggs and Rum"

•

To some traditionalists, including myself, Christmas would not be the same—in fact would be rather bleak—without a huge punch bowl of eggnog. Eggnog is descended from the old English concoction "sack posset," a hot drink of ale, rum, eggs, and milk. "Nog" is an Old English word for a strong ale, and since eggs were such an important part of the punch, it became known as "eggnog." Eggnog became especially popular in the winter months when fresh fruit juices to mix with liquors were not readily available, and because of its "celebratory" effects it became an essential part of the holiday ritual.

Joe's Lentil Soup

My friend Joe Brescia makes good use of a ham bone by cooking up a big pot of this Italian lentil soup. This thick, hearty dish is a wonderful main course on a cold winter's night served with a green salad and a whole wheat Italian bread. This soup freezes well.

2 cups dried lentils, picked over and washed well
1 meaty ham bone
1 medium yellow onion, chopped
2 quarts water
4 to 5 large garlic cloves
1 bunch Italian parsley
1 cup tomato puree
¼ cup olive oil
½ teaspoon dried oregano
¾ cup tubetti or other small pasta
Salt and freshly ground black pepper
Grated Locatelli, Romano, or Parmesan cheese

1. Place the lentils, ham bone, chopped onion, and 2 quarts water in a large stockpot and bring to a boil over medium heat. Turn off the heat, cover the pot, and soak for 1 hour. Bring to a boil again and simmer for about 1 hour, or until the lentils are tender.

2. Remove the ham bone from the pot and cut off any chunks of meat left on the bone. Toss these back in the pot and discard the bone.

3. Chop the garlic and parsley together in the bowl of a food processor or chop by hand with a sharp knife. Add this, along with the tomato puree, olive oil, and oregano to the pot. Simmer over low heat for about 30 minutes.

4. In a separate pot, boil the pasta in salted water until it is *al dente.* Drain the pasta and stir it into the soup at the end of the 30 minutes simmering time.

5. Season the soup with salt and plenty of freshly ground pepper. Serve in large shallow bowls and pass a bowl of grated cheese.

A DICKENSIAN DINNER

•

FOR 8 TO 10

MENU

Juniper's Gin Punch

Roasted Chestnuts

Roasted Goose with Sage and Scallion Dressing

Johnny's Applesauce   Sautéed Red Cabbage

Sugarplum Pudding (page 16) with Spiced Brandy Butter

British Cheeses with "Biscuits"

This menu is a step back in time to the Victorian era in England, when much of our Anglo-American Christmas traditions began. The Victorians were the ones who turned Christmas, previously mainly a religious observance, into a glorious celebration with holly and mistletoe, roving carolers, gaily decorated Christmas trees and spectacular feasts.

Many of us wouldn't want to let Christmas go by without enjoying a crisp, succulent, fragrant, Christmas goose. This rich and inviting dinner is based on the dinner served for Christmas at the humble home of Bob Cratchit.

The Cratchits had mashed potatoes with gravy, but I like to serve the gravy with the meat and dressing and dispense with the potatoes altogether. Here, they've been replaced by a simple Sautéed Red Cabbage, which is not only a tasty addition to the menu, but

" 'There never was such a goose.' Bob said he didn't believe there ever was such a goose cooked."

Charles Dickens
A Christmas Carol

" 'Oh! What a wonderful pudding!' Bob Cratchit said, and calmly too, that he regarded it as the greatest success achieved by Mrs. Cratchit since their marriage."

Charles Dickens
A Christmas Carol

119

adds color and crunch. The applesauce is probably not as Mrs. Cratchit made it—this is my own rather unorthodox method for a savory, less sweet sauce.

Alas, the Cratchits almost certainly went without the luxury of rich Brandy Butter on their Christmas pudding, but they did follow up the pudding with fresh fruit. You may want to put out a bowl of apples and oranges at the end of the meal as they did.

Getting Ready: This is not a difficult menu to prepare, especially since the Sugarplum Pudding was made long ago and stored away to ripen. Put it on to steam for serving about 2 hours before your plan to serve it.

The punch can be mixed in only a few minutes just before serving; make the ice ring a day before and chill the ingredients a few hours in advance. The chestnuts can be roasted out of the kitchen by the children (with supervision) over the fire, or they can be popped in and out of the oven while the goose is roasting.

The Sage and Scallion Dressing requires little time and can be made early in the day with bread crumbs prepared several days ahead and stored tightly covered. Don't mix the dressing or stuff the goose, however, until just before putting into the oven. Allow 20 to 25 minutes per pound for roasting the goose.

Johnny's Applesauce and Spiced Brandy Butter can be prepared several days ahead and refrigerated. Warm up the applesauce in a heavy saucepan just before serving.

For the Sautéed Red Cabbage, shred and blanch the cabbage up to a day ahead of time and store, tightly wrapped in the refrigerator. About 10 minutes before serving time, you need to begin cooking it—just after the goose comes out of the oven to rest.

Beverages: The punch should be served before dinner, with the Roasted Chestnuts if you like, and not during the meal. A nice wine to go with the goose would be a Gewurtztraminer if you like white, or a Gamay if you prefer red.

Setting: Here's the chance to cover the table with Victorian splendor. Use a lace tablecloth and lace-trimmed napkins, and get out great-grandma's china and crystal and sterling silver flatware. Arrange pink sweetheart roses, holly, and baby's breath tied with rose pink and moss green velvet ribbons in a crystal bowl at the center of the table. Let the tails of the ribbons run to the corners of the table and trail over the edges (pin them discreetly to the cloth). Arrange a row of lace fans (or fans made from paper doilies) and holly down the center of the table, along with gaudy silver candlesticks fitted with soft pink candles. To complete the ambience, play albums of Old English carols.

Roasted Chestnuts

•

Here's a method for roasting chestnuts in the oven that makes it easy to peel these ornery critters.

Preheat the oven to 375°F. With a sharp knife cut a cross into the flat side of each chestnut, then spread them on a greased baking sheet and roast for 5 to 7 minutes, or until the skins can be removed easily. Dump the chestnuts into a wooden bowl or a basket and put out an extra bowl for the shells. Serve hot and let everyone peel his or her own.

Juniper's Gin Punch

MAKES ABOUT 18 SERVINGS

MAKES ABOUT 18 SERVINGS

This cold punch is not too sweet and is a good lead-in to the goose.

1 orange
2 limes
3 cups gin, chilled
2 cups apricot brandy, chilled
2 liters club soda, chilled
12 ounces frozen orange juice concentrate

1. Slice the orange and limes into thin round slices and line a 4-cup round mold with the slices. Carefully fill the mold with cold water and place in the freezer. Freeze until solid.

2. Combine the remaining ingredients in a punch bowl and stir to blend. Unmold the ice ring and carefully float it in the punch bowl, fruited side up.

Roasted Goose with Sage and Scallion Dressing

SERVES 8 TO 10

1 cup (2 sticks) butter
12 scallions, white and green parts, thinly sliced
1 medium onion, chopped
1 cup chopped celery
1 small apple, coarsely chopped
6 cups coarse dry bread crumbs
½ teaspoon salt
1 teaspoon freshly ground black pepper
2 tablespoons chopped fresh sage *or* 1 tablespoon dried sage
1 teaspoon dried thyme
2 tablespoons chopped parsley
½ cup chicken stock
2 large eggs, lightly beaten

1 12- to 14-pound goose
Fruity white wine *or* cider, for basting

1. Melt the butter in a skillet and add the scallions, onion, celery, and apple. Sauté about 10 minutes, or until the onion is transparent and golden brown.

2. Transfer to a large mixing bowl and add the bread crumbs, salt, pepper, and herbs. Toss to combine well; then add the chicken stock and eggs. Toss again to combine all ingredients. Add a bit more stock if the stuffing seems too dry.

3. Preheat the oven to 450°F. Rinse and dry the goose and season the cavity with salt and pepper. Stuff the goose loosely with the dressing and truss using trussing skewers and string. Prick the exterior of the goose all over with a sharp-tined fork to allow excess fat to escape during roasting.

4. Place the goose on a rack in a large, deep roasting pan, breast side up. Place in the oven and roast for 15 minutes; then lower the oven temperature to 350°F. Continue roasting for about 20 minutes a pound, or until the goose is very well browned and the leg joints move up and down easily. During the roasting time remove any fat that accumulates in the pan and baste with white wine or cider.

5. When the goose is done, remove it to a board and let it rest, loosely covered with aluminum foil, for ½ hour before carving. Make the gravy (recipe follows) while the goose is resting.

Goose Gravy
¼ cup goose fat
¼ cup all-purpose flour
4 cups chicken stock
Pan drippings and scrapings
Salt and freshly ground black pepper to taste

1. When removing the goose fat from the pan during roasting, reserve ¼ cup. Place in a heavy saucepan over medium heat and slowly stir in the flour. Cook slowly, stirring frequently, until a brown roux has formed. Add the chicken stock a cup at a time, stirring constantly. Simmer about 5 to 7 minutes, or until the flour is cooked and the gravy is thickened.

2. When the goose comes out of the pan, pour off the fat; then pour off the remaining drippings and any scraped browned bits from the pan into the gravy. Stir to blend thoroughly and season with salt and pepper to taste.

The Goose Club

•

One of the great Victorian working-class institutions was the goose club, much like our modern-day Christmas clubs. By contributing a small part of his week's wages to his goose club, even the everyday working man could afford to buy his family a goose for Christmas dinner.

Johnny's Applesauce

This is not a conventional method for making applesauce—the apples are sautéed with butter and onions before being pureed, then spiked currants are stirred in. This not-too-sweet sauce is delicious served warm with poultry and pork.

½ cup dried currants
⅓ cup Calvados *or* applejack
1 medium onion, coarsely chopped
¼ cup (½ stick) butter
8 large tart apples
¼ teaspoon grated lemon rind
1 to 2 tablespoons sugar, or to taste

1. Place the currants and Calvados or applejack in a small bowl and let steep for 2 hours at room temperature. Stir occasionally.

2. Place the onion and butter in a large skillet over medium heat and sauté until the onion is transparent, about 15 minutes.

3. While the onion is sautéing, peel, core, and coarsely chop the apples. Add the apples to the skillet and toss together with the onion. Cover the skillet and sauté until the apples are tender, stirring occasionally, about 15 minutes. Stir in the lemon rind and sugar to taste—the sauce should not be too sweet.

4. Remove the mixture from the heat and puree in batches in the bowl of a food processor fitted with a chopping blade. Stir in the currants and liquid with a spoon. Serve immediately or cover, cool, and chill; then reheat in a heavy saucepan before serving.

Sautéed Red Cabbage

SERVES 8 TO 10

1 2-pound red cabbage, cored and coarsely shredded
4 tablespoons lemon juice
¼ cup (½ stick) butter
2 teaspoons sugar
1 teaspoon caraway seeds
Salt and freshly ground black pepper

1. Place the cabbage in a large pot of boiling salted water and add 2 tablespoons lemon juice. Bring to a boil and boil for 2 to 3 minutes. Drain well and rinse with cold water. (The dish may be prepared ahead up to this point.)

2. Melt the butter in a large skillet over medium heat; then stir in the remaining 2 tablespoons lemon juice, butter, sugar, and caraway seeds. Add the cabbage to the skillet and sauté for 5 to 7 minutes, or until the cabbage is crisp-tender. Season with salt and freshly ground black pepper to taste, and serve in a warmed vegetable bowl.

Spiced Brandy Butter

MAKES ABOUT 1¼ CUPS

¾ cup (1½ sticks) butter, softened
½ cup sifted confectioners' sugar
¼ cup brandy
¼ teaspoon ground ginger
¼ teaspoon ground cinnamon

1. Beat all the ingredients together in a small mixing bowl until smooth. Cover and chill until firm but still pliable.

2. Use a butter mold to make individual servings or a butter curler to make curls. Chill in ice water until firm and serve drained portions in a chilled serving dish. *Or* shape the brandy butter into a cylinder about 1½ inches in diameter and about 6 inches long and wrap in wax paper or plastic wrap, then chill until firm. To serve, slice ½-inch-thick slices from the brandy butter log.

A NOUVELLE NOËL DINNER

•

FOR 8

MENU

White Christmas Soup

Grilled Pork Medallions with Pear and Tangerine Chutney

Sautéed Sweet Potato Julienne

Snow Peas in Black Butter

Roasted Red and Green Pepper Salad

Applejack-Roasted Apples with Crème Fraîche

Spiced Coffee

*T*his menu owes as much to the adventurous yet tradition-bound spirit of the New American Cuisine as to the discipline of Nouvelle Cuisine (there are no sauce puddles here!), but I couldn't resist using this name. There are influences here from many cuisines—a hint of Indian curry in the soup, Oriental snow peas sautéed in a classic French black butter—but the end result is distinctly American. Here's a perfect menu to serve when you don't want to spend a lot of time in the kitchen making Christmas dinner and you'd like dinner to have a lighter touch than a more traditional feast.

Getting Ready: The day before you can do the following: make the soup and the chutney, roast the peppers and make the dress-

"At a dinner party one should eat wisely but not too well, and talk well but not too wisely."

W. Somerset Maugham

125

ing for the salad, and roast the apples. The crème fraîche for the apples needs to be started at least two days before serving.

The pork medallions, sweet potatoes, and snow peas should be made just before serving, but won't keep you in the kitchen for more than 30 minutes. After putting on the soup to reheat slowly, blanch the sweet potatoes and then brush the pork medallions with oil. Next begin warming the chutney. While the pork is broiling, trim and sauté the snow peas and the sweet potatoes. Once the pork comes out of the broiler, pop the apples into the oven to warm up. While you're preparing the main course, enlist a volunteer to arrange the salad on individual plates; then have the volunteer help in arranging the individual dinner plates.

Beverages: I'd skip wine with the creamy soup, but if you'd like to start with a wine before and during this course, try a Chenin Blanc. I like a light, fruity Zinfandel with the pork, but if you prefer a white wine try a dry Chardonnay or a less dry Chenin Blanc from California. Spiced coffee with dessert and a Late Harvest Riesling afterward finish this dinner off nicely.

Setting: I like to serve this menu dramatically against an all-white background. The first course is pale, and then the table blooms with a succession of colors—the food. I set the table with a white-on-white damask cloth and white napkins. At each place, set with simple bold-banded white china, simple silverware, and elegant crystal, I place a small white votive candle in a plain glass holder. In the center of the table are several small white poinsettia plants in white pots.

Menu Variations: The Cream of Mushroom and Onion Soup (page 40) from the Thanksgiving dinner would work well here, and if fresh snow peas are unavailable, try sautéed zucchini slices. Try a green salad with olive oil and balsamic vinegar and crumbled goat cheese, and for dessert, the Apple–Ginger Sorbet from the Tree-Trimming Buffet (page 64).

"A cheerful look makes a dish a feast."
George Herbert

White Christmas Soup

SERVES 8

¾ cup (1½ sticks) butter
2 garlic cloves
2 medium onions, chopped
6 large leeks, white parts only, cleaned well and chopped
1 teaspoon curry powder
2½ pounds bay scallops, rinsed well
2 cups chicken stock
2 large egg yolks
1 cup heavy cream
2½ cups milk
Salt
Snipped chives
Cayenne pepper

1. In a large heavy saucepan over medium heat, melt the butter and add the garlic, onions, leeks, and curry powder. Sautéed about 15 minutes, or until the onions are translucent and tender. Remove the garlic cloves and discard them.

2. Stir in the scallops and chicken stock. Bring to a simmer and cook about 10 minutes, or until the scallops are snow white and opaque. Turn the heat to low.

3. Pour the soup into the bowl of a food processor fitted with a metal chopping blade and puree, in batches if necessary. Return the soup to the pot and keep warm over very low heat.

4. In a small mixing bowl, beat the egg yolks together with the cream and milk. Slowly stir this mixture into the soup. Continue cooking the soup over low heat, stirring constantly, until it thickens slightly. Do not boil. Season the soup with salt to taste.

5. Serve the soup hot, garnished with snipped chives and a pinch of cayenne pepper.

Grilled Pork Medallions with Pear and Tangerine Chutney

The subtle combination of pears and tangerines makes for a not-too-sweet accent to grilled or broiled pork. Try the chutney with duck or country ham, too. The chutney can be made up to 2 days ahead and stored in a covered jar in the refrigerator. Simply warm it up in a heavy pan just before serving.

2 tablespoons butter
1 small onion, chopped
2 medium shallots, finely chopped
1 tablespoon finely chopped gingerroot
¼ cup dry white wine
2 tablespoons sugar
1 tangerine, peeled, seeded, and white membranes removed, coarsely chopped
2 firm ripe pears, peeled and coarsely chopped
Grated rind of ½ tangerine
⅛ teaspoon cayenne pepper
16 pork loin medallions
Vegetable oil
Salt

1. To make the chutney, melt the butter in a small heavy saucepan over medium heat; then add the onion and shallots. Sauté about 10 minutes, or until the onion becomes transparent.

2. Add the gingerroot, wine, and sugar, stir and bring to a boil. Simmer for 10 minutes, or until thick. Add the tangerine, pears, grated tangerine rind, and cayenne; then bring to a boil again and simmer about 10 minutes, or until the pears are just tender, but not mushy. Stir occasionally to prevent sticking.

3. Preheat the broiler. Brush the pork medallions on each side lightly with vegetable oil. Season with a small amount of salt. Broil the medallions about 3 to 4 minutes per side, or until just cooked through.

4. To serve, arrange 2 medallions next to each other on each plate. Spoon a small ribbon of warm chutney across the medallions and pass additional chutney in a small serving dish.

Sautéed Sweet Potato Julienne

SERVES 8

Sweet potatoes are served too infrequently. There's nothing more comforting than a simple baked sweet potato slathered with gobs of sweet butter and a grinding of pepper. This method of fixing sweet potatoes is equally delicious, and makes a delicate accompaniment to the pork.

1½ pounds sweet potatoes, peeled and cut into ⅛-inch julienne
2 teaspoons salt
¼ cup (½ stick) butter
Freshly ground black pepper

1. Place the julienned sweet potatoes in a saucepan with the salt and cover with water. Bring to a boil and cook for 5 minutes. Drain.

2. Melt the butter in a skillet over medium heat. Add the sweet potatoes and toss. Sauté for 3 to 5 minutes, or until the sweet potatoes golden brown. Remove the sweet potatoes from the pan with a slotted spoon and place on paper towels for a few seconds to absorb the excess butter.

3. Serve in small mounds on one side of the pork medallions, and top with a grinding of pepper.

Snow Peas in Black Butter

SERVES 8

Black butter (beurre noir) is not really black at all, despite its name. The browned butter gives the crisp snow peas a nice, nutty flavor.

2 pounds snow peas
¼ cup (½ stick) butter
1 teaspoon lemon juice
1 tablespoon chopped parsley

1. Trim the snow peas and cut them in half on the diagonal.

2. In a medium heavy skillet, melt the butter over medium heat. Continue cooking until the butter begins to darken and foam. Stir in the lemon juice, parsley, and snow peas and sauté for 2 to 3 minutes, or until the snow peas turn a bright emerald green. Do not overcook—snow peas should be served crisp.

Roasted Red and Green Pepper Salad

SERVES 8

3 large green peppers, roasted and peeled (page 90)
2 large red peppers, roasted and peeled (page 90)
2 garlic cloves
Red Wine Vinaigrette (page 147)
3 heads Boston lettuce, washed and dried

1. Seed the peppers and cut them vertically into ½-inch strips. Place the peppers in a small bowl with the garlic cloves and Red Wine Vinaigrette to cover. Cover tightly with plastic wrap and marinate in the refrigerator for 1 hour.

2. Remove the pepper strips from the dressing and drain in a colander. Discard the garlic cloves.

3. Line eight salad plates with the lettuce leaves. Arrange the pepper strips, alternating the colors, in a fan shape on each plate, and serve.

Spiced Coffee

●

Whenever I serve this coffee, it's always greeted with oohs and aahs, yet making it is simplicity itself. Add ½ teaspoon ground cinnamon, ½ teaspoon ground allspice, and a pinch of nutmeg to the filter basket when making a 10- to 12-cup pot of coffee.

Applejack-Roasted Apples

SERVES 8

This "inebriated" version of the classic baked apple has no spices, allowing the flavors of the simple, basic ingredients to shine. Choose tart baking apples, such as Cortlands, Baldwins, or Granny Smiths. If crème fraîche is un-available, a method for making mock crème fraîche at the end of the recipe is quite a good stand-in. Or serve the apples with sweet-ened whipped cream flavored with a few tablespoons of applejack.

½ cup chopped pecans *or* walnuts
½ cup golden raisins
1¼ cups sugar
1 cup applejack
¼ cup (½ stick) butter
8 tart baking apples

1. Preheat the oven to 350°F. In a small bowl, combine the nuts and raisins and set aside.

2. In a small heavy saucepan, combine the sugar, applejack, and butter. Bring to a boil, lower the heat, and simmer for about 5 minutes.

3. Core and peel the apples halfway down from the stem end, leaving the peel on the bottom half. Stand the apples in a shallow baking pan just big enough to hold them, and fill the center of each with the nut-raisin mixture. Pour the syrup over and into the apples.

4. Roast the apples for 40 to 50 minutes, basting with the syrup every 15 minutes. When the apples are tender, remove them from the oven and cool for 1 hour before serving. Or cool, cover well, and refrigerate; then reheat in a slow oven.

5. Serve the apples in small shallow bowls with the syrup spooned over each one and a dollop of crème fraîche.

Crème Fraîche

MAKES 2 CUPS

1 cup heavy cream
1 cup sour cream

1. Combine the two creams in a large covered jar or a tightly covered bowl and allow to stand at room temperature for 12 hours or overnight, until the mixture thickens.

2. Stir again and refrigerate for at least 24 hours before using. This will keep for about a week, covered and refrigerated.

A FEAST FIT FOR A KING

•

FOR 8 TO 10

MENU

Potted Shrimp with Scallions and Dill

Standing Rib Roast of Beef au Poivre with Sauce Diabolique

Cheshire Pudding

Brussels Sprouts with Chestnuts

Chelsea Chocolate Trifle

*T*his savory dinner, with a peppery rib roast standing front and center, will satisfy the heartiest eaters. The menu is English in inspiration, with some spicy overtones from a bit farther south. The trifle, which answers the all-American craving for chocolate, is named for Manhattan's Chelsea, where I live, rather than London's Chelsea, in the mother country of trifle. This is a somewhat pricey menu, but Christmas does only come once a year.

Getting Ready: The first thing to do is to order your rib roast about a week in advance. As far as the cooking is concerned, there is a bit of last-minute preparation here, but it should take less than half an hour.

The Potted Shrimp has to be made a day in advance. The cake for the trifle can be made ahead, too, as can the custard, but wait to assemble the trifle until early on the day it is to be served. The trifle should be assembled early in the day, except for the whipping and layering of the cream, which should be done no more than a few hours ahead.

132

The roast beef requires several hours in the oven, and is sometimes a bit unpredictable, so try to be ready when it is. Check the recipe for timing according to the size of your roast and how well done you like it. When the roast comes out of the oven to rest, raise the oven temperature for the Cheshire Pudding. There is plenty of time to bake the pudding, and then make the Sauce Diabolique.

The chestnuts can be boiled and peeled early in the day; then they can be put on to steam with the Brussels sprouts about 20 minutes before serving.

Beverages: Serve glasses of dry sherry before dinner. Try a Sauvignon Blanc or Chardonnay with the shrimp, and with the main course, a good California Merlot or Cabernet Sauvignon, which are my favorites with beef. With the trifle, serve very strong coffee and an assortment of liqueurs.

Setting: This is an all-out, once-a-year formal dinner, and the table setting should reflect it. Use your very best white or gold damask table cloth and napkins, and your heirloom china, crystal, and flatware. For a centerpiece, fill a footed crystal or silver bowl with shiny red apples and nuts with sprigs of holly drooping down the sides. Fit 12-inch red or gold tapered candles into your most elaborate candelabra.

Menu Variations: As first course alternates, other choices might be the Smoked Salmon with Horseradish-Mustard Cream (page 164) or the Onion-Rosemary Tartlets (page 72), which could be served with predinner drinks. Sautéed julienned carrots would be a good substitute side dish for those who don't like Brussels sprouts and/or chestnuts. Almost any dessert from the Dessert Party menu (pages 151–161) could be substituted for the trifle, as long as it's rich and gooey.

"Heap on more wood!—the wind is chill;
But let it whistle as it will;
We'll keep our Christmas merry still.
Sir Walter Scott

Potted Shrimp
with Scallions and Dill

SERVES 8 TO 10 AS A FIRST COURSE,
18 TO 20 AS AN HORS D'OEUVRE

Potted shrimp spread onto slivers of toast is a great treat but seems a bit bland to our modern palates; this version livens it up a bit. Even though the shrimp are chopped, don't use tiny ones as they tend to toughen in cooking.

1½ pounds medium shrimp
3 scallions, white and green parts, finely chopped
1 tablespoon finely chopped dill
¼ cup lemon juice
½ teaspoon grated lemon rind
Several pinches of cayenne pepper
1 cup (2 sticks) butter
Dill sprigs
Melba Toasts (page 195)

1. Cover the shrimp with water in a saucepan and bring to a boil. Cook the shrimp until they are just pink. Drain and cool.

2. Peel and devein the shrimp, reserving the shells. Chop the shrimp very fine and combine in a mixing bowl with the scallions, dill, lemon juice, and lemon rind. Add a few dashes of cayenne and mix well. Put the mixture in a crock or deep bowl.

3. Melt the butter in a small skillet over low heat. Chop up the shrimp shells and add them to the skillet. Sauté over low heat for about 10 minutes, watching so the butter does not brown.

4. Strain the butter through cheesecloth into a spouted cup or bowl; then pour the butter over the shrimp mixture to cover. Cool to room temperature; then cover with aluminum foil or plastic wrap and chill overnight before serving.

5. To serve as an hors d'oeuvre, place the uncovered crock on a platter and garnish with dill sprigs. Surround the crock with small slices of white melba toast. To serve as a first course on individual plates, place a small mound on a Boston lettuce leaf on each plate and top the mound with a dill sprig. Arrange 4 to 5 thin slices of toast on one side.

Standing Rib Roast of Beef *au Poivre*

SERVES 8 TO 10

About ½ cup whole black peppercorns
1 5- to 6-pound standing rib roast of beef, at room temperature

1. Preheat the oven to the 475°F. Place the peppercorns in a small heavy brown bag and crush by banging with a mallet. With the palm of your hand, press the peppercorns into all surfaces of the meat.

2. Place the roast, fat side up, on a rack in a shallow roasting pan; then put into the oven and roast for 30 minutes.

3. Lower the oven temperature to 300°F. Baste the roast with the pan juices and insert a meat thermometer into the thickest part of the roast, making sure that the thermometer does not touch the bone.

4. Continue roasting for about 30 minutes and check the thermometer reading. Roast until the thermometer reads 135°F. for rare (about 16 minutes per pound total roasting time) to 160°F. for medium-well (about 25 minutes per pound total roasting time). When desired doneness is reached, remove it from the oven and allow it to rest, loosely covered with aluminum foil, about 30 minutes before carving. Prepare the Sauce Diabolique (recipe follows).

5. To serve, carve into ¼ to ½-inch-thick slices and ladle a few tablespoons of the sauce onto each serving.

"The damsel donn'd her kirtle sheen;
The hall was dress'd with holly green;
Forth to the wood did merry men go,
To gather in the mistletoe."
Sir Walter Scott

Sauce Diabolique

MAKES ABOUT 2 CUPS

²⁄₃ cup dry red wine
1 cup pan juices from beef roast and/or beef stock
1 teaspoon whole black peppercorns, crushed
1 tablespoon dry mustard
2 tablespoons chopped parsley
2 tablespoons finely chopped shallots
2 tablespoons prepared horseradish

1. Combine the red wine and pan juices in a small saucepan and place over medium heat. Stir in the peppercorns and dry mustard, bring to a boil, and simmer for about 5 minutes.

2. Stir in the remaining ingredients and serve immediately in a warmed gravy boat or small serving bowl.

Cheshire Pudding

SERVES 8 TO 10

4 large eggs
2 cups milk
2 cups all-purpose flour
½ teaspoon salt
½ cup pan drippings from rib roast
½ cup grated Cheshire cheese

1. After removing the roast from the oven, raise the oven temperature to 450°F. Place a 9 × 13-inch shallow baking pan in the oven to heat up.

2. Beat the eggs until light and fluffy; then beat in the milk. Sift together the flour and salt; then beat into the egg-milk mixture until the batter is just smooth.

3. Remove the baking pan from the oven and pour in the pan drippings. Pour the batter over the drippings, sprinkle the grated cheese over the batter, and quickly place the pan in the oven. Bake for 10 minutes.

This piquant sauce is also excellent with broiled steaks and chops.

"Woe to the cook whose sauce has no sting!"
Chaucer

This variation of Yorkshire pudding is made zesty by the addition of grated Cheshire cheese. If Cheshire cheese is unavailable, substitute a sharp Cheddar. To make traditional Yorkshire pudding, simply omit the cheese.

4. Without opening the oven, lower the temperature to 375°F. and continue baking for about 15 minutes, or until the pudding is puffed and lightly browned. Cut into 12 approximately 3-inch squares and serve immediately with the roast.

Brussels Sprouts with Chestnuts

SERVES 8 TO 10

2 10-ounce containers Brussels sprouts
1 pound chestnuts
2 tablespoons butter
6 thin slices bacon, cooked, drained, and crumbled
Salt and freshly ground black pepper

1. To pare the chestnuts, cut crosses onto the flat sides of the chestnuts with a sharp paring knife. Drop the chestnuts into a pot of boiling water and boil for about 15 minutes. Remove a few at a time and peel off the outer and inner skins. If the skins are too difficult to remove, boil a few minutes longer.

2. While the chestnuts are boiling, prepare the Brussels sprouts: remove any discolored outer leaves, trim and score each root end with an X, and wash carefully under cold running water to remove any sandy particles.

3. Place the chestnuts in a vegetable steamer over boiling water and steam for 10 minutes. Add the sprouts and steam about 7 minutes, or until the sprouts are crisp-tender and bright green.

4. Remove the Brussels sprouts and chestnuts to a warmed vegetable bowl and toss with butter, crumbled bacon, and salt and pepper to taste. Serve hot.

Chelsea Chocolate Trifle

SERVES 10

By adding chocolate to the cake, this pretty and impressive concoction takes the traditional trifle one step beyond its usual boozy and creamy sinfulness. The one never-to-be broken rule in trifle making, however, is that it must be assembled in your prettiest glass bowl— a footed fruit bowl works perfectly, or a huge brandy snifter, or a real trifle bowl if you happen to have one. Don't be scared off by the length of this recipe—the cake can be made 2 or 3 days ahead and the custard the day before assembling the trifle.

Chocolate Sponge Cake
8 ounces unsweetened chocolate
6 large eggs, at room temperature
1 cup sugar
1½ teaspoons vanilla extract
1 teaspoon baking powder
¼ teaspoon salt
¾ cup cake flour

1. Preheat the oven to 350°F. Grease two 9-inch square cake pans, line the bottoms with wax paper, then butter the wax paper.

2. Melt the chocolate in the top of a double boiler over simmering water; remove from the heat and allow to cool.

3. Separate the eggs into 2 large mixing bowls. Beat the egg yolks until thick and lemon-colored. Gradually beat in ¾ cup sugar and then the vanilla. Stir in the melted and cooled chocolate.

4. In another bowl, beat the egg whites until stiff peaks form, then beat in the remaining ¼ cup sugar. Gently fold about one-quarter of the egg whites into the yolk-chocolate mixture. Spoon the remaining egg whites onto the chocolate mixture.

5. Sift together the baking powder, salt, and cake flour, then sift this mixture over the egg whites. Fold all together gently until the whites and flour mixture are just blended into the yolk-chocolate mixture.

6. Spoon the batter into the prepared cake pans and bake until a cake tester or toothpick inserted in the center of the layers comes out clean, about 35 minutes. Remove from the oven and invert the layers onto wire racks. Allow the layers to cool completely before removing the pans.

Custard
4 cups milk
6 large egg yolks
½ cup sugar
¼ teaspoon salt
1½ teaspoons vanilla extract

1. Pour the milk into the top of a double boiler over simmering water and bring to just below the simmering point.

2. While the milk is heating, beat the egg yolks, sugar, and salt together in a mixing bowl until the yolks thicken and lighten in color. Gradually pour the hot milk into this mixture, beating continuously.

3. Pour the mixture back into the top of the double boiler and cook, stirring continuously, until the custard has thickened and thickly coats the back of the spoon. *Do not allow to simmer at any point.*

4. Remove the top of the double boiler from the heat and dip it into a large bowl of cold water to stop the custard from cooking any further. Beat the custard briskly for 5 minutes to help it cool off rapidly; then beat in the vanilla. Cool the custard completely; then store, tightly covered, in the refrigerator until assembling the trifle.

Assembly
¾ cup raspberry preserves
¾ cup toasted slivered almonds
1 cup Chambord raspberry liqueur
½ cup dry sherry
2 cups heavy cream
2 tablespoons confectioners' sugar
½ teaspoon vanilla extract
Pinch of salt
Shaved chocolate curls

1. Spread the tops of the two sponge cake layers evenly with preserves. Sprinkle ½ cup almonds onto one layer. Place the layers atop each other, preserves-coated sides together, and press gently together.

2. Cut the sandwiched cake layers into fingers, about 1 × 3 inches. Arrange the layers in the bottom and partially up the sides of a glass serving bowl 10 to 12 inches in diameter and 4 to 5 inches deep. Pour liqueur and sherry evenly over the cake and allow to absorb about 10 minutes; then spoon the cooled custard over, covering the cake completely. (The trifle may be made ahead up to this point, covered, and chilled.)

3. Whip the cream in a chilled bowl until stiff peaks form. Beat in the sugar, vanilla, and salt. Spoon the whipped cream onto the

"Life is a banquet and most poor suckers are starving."
Rosalind Russell as Auntie Mame

trifle in mounds, completely covering the custard. Garnish with the remaining slivered almonds and shaved chocolate curls. Serve with big spoons and a smile.

Double Trouble Trifle Add 1 ounce unsweetened chocolate while heating the milk in making the custard.

Traditional Trifle Substitute yellow sponge cake or 1 dozen split ladyfingers for the chocolate sponge cake and use sherry or rum instead of the liqueur.

Other Variations Any fruit preserves can be substituted for the raspberry preserves along with a corresponding liqueur, e.g., cherry preserves and Kirsch, orange marmalade and Grand Marnier, or pear preserves and pear brandy. Sweetened ripe banana puree mixed with a bit of lemon juice also makes a delicious filling—douse the cake with rum. A summer trifle can be made with sweetened crushed berries, plums, or peaches.

"To some fanciers of trifle, its most important aspect is its function as a vehicle for spirits. Recently at a dinner I attended the chef had been more than usually generous with their application, and when the trifle appeared at table a young lady was heard to exclaim after the first bite: 'This is an *especially* fine trifle!' "
William Barnard

AN ALL-AMERICAN OPEN HOUSE BUFFET DINNER

•

FOR 18 TO 20

MENU

Twin Turkey Roulades

Old-Fashioned Fresh Cranberry Relish

Puree of Yellow Winter Vegetables

Puree of White Winter Vegetables

Marinated Broccoli Salad

Pumpkin–Praline Cheesecake

Steamed Ginger Pudding with Cranberry Fool

"Now Christmas is come. Let us beat up the drum, and call all our neighbors to-gether."
Washington Irving

On the rare occasions when we haven't gone home to Ohio for Christmas, we invite our extended family of friends who might otherwise be spending Christmas alone over for a big buffet dinner. Each person is asked to bring a grab bag gift with a five-dollar price limit. As each guest arrives, a numbered label is attached to each gift and it's placed under the tree. Between the main course and dessert, everyone pulls a number from Santa's hat and we all open our gifts.

Getting Ready: The only dishes that need to be made just before serving are the two vegetable purees, but they require very little time away from your guests if the vegetables have been chopped early in the day and stored, covered with water and tightly covered, in the refrigerator.

The Turkey Roulades are best made a day ahead, and the Cranberry Relish should be made two or three days in advance.

No more than one day ahead, make the broccoli salad, steam the Ginger Pudding, and bake the Pumpkin–Praline Cheesecake. The Cranberry Fool is best made no sooner than early on the day it is served.

Beverages: Offer guests a choice of several American wines: a Chardonnay, a dry Grenache rosé, or a Gamay or light Zinfandel. Serve a Late Harvest Zinfandel after dessert.

Setting: I like to cover the buffet table with a red-and-green-plaid tablecloth and arrange a grouping from the collection of antique and folk art Santa Clauses I've been adding to for years with fat red candles for a centerpiece. Plates are placed on a nearby sideboard, along with flatware rolled up in white napkins and tied with plaid ribbons.

For music on Christmas Day, just turn on the radio, since many stations play seasonal music all day long.

Menu Variations: With two desserts at the end of the meal, there's really no need to serve anything at the beginning. But if you feel it is necessary, serve the Cheddar Cheese Straws (page 39) or small Jalapeño–Cornmeal Biscuits (page 45), split and layered with thin slices of ham and Hot Honey Mustard (page 24), or a small bowl of nuts with before-dinner drinks.

An alternative to the vegetable purees is Steamed Brussels Sprouts and Carrots with Two Mustards (double the recipe on page 43), in which case a simple green salad should be served rather than the broccoli salad. In varying this menu, remember to serve only dishes that won't become messy looking when served buffet style.

"The Christmas fires
brightly burn
and dance among
the holly boughs,
The Christmas pudding's spicy steam
with fragrance
fills the house,
While merry glows
each friendly soul
over the foaming
wassail bowl."
Anne P. L. Field

Twin Turkey Roulades

SERVES 18 TO 20

I call this "Tom's Turkey," so named for my friend Tom Barnes, who created it. This is a perfect buffet main course, with turkey and stuffing all rolled into one and then cut into neat spiraled slices. An added plus is that guests have their choice of two roulades, one white meat and the other dark. This is best when made a day in advance.

1 14- to 15-pound turkey
1 pound bulk sausage
6 eggs
¼ cup chopped parsley
1 teaspoon salt
1 teaspoon freshly ground black pepper
1 teaspoon dried savory
1 teaspoon dried chervil
1 small onion, finely chopped
¼ cup (½ stick) butter, softened

1. Skin the turkey carefully by slipping a sharp knife gently between the skin and the flesh. Try to leave the skin in as large pieces as possible.

2. Cut away the white and dark meats in chunks (this doesn't have to be done too carefully), and divide the meat into two large mixing bowls, one for the white meat and one for the dark. Even out the quantity in each bowl by putting some of the white meat in with the dark.

3. Coarsely chop the meat separately in the bowl of a food processor fitted with the steel chopping blade. Return the meat to the separate mixing bowls and divide the remaining ingredients except the butter between the bowls. Add the butter to the bowl containing the white meat. Using your hands, mix the ingredients of each bowl as you would mix a pâté or meat loaf until well blended.

4. Line two jelly roll pans with aluminum foil and oil the foil lightly. Place each mixture onto one of the pans and press each into an even rectangular layer about ½ inch thick. Cover each pan loosely and refrigerate for 1 hour. While the meat is chilling, make the stuffing (following page).

Stuffing
¾ cup wild rice
3 celery stalks, finely chopped
6 scallions, finely chopped
3 tablespoons butter
1 large garlic clove, finely chopped
½ cup finely chopped parsley
½ teaspoon dried savory
¼ teaspoon dried sage
¼ teaspoon dried thyme
¼ teaspoon salt
¼ teaspoon freshly ground black pepper
3 cups fine fresh bread crumbs
2 large eggs, lightly beaten
½ cup heavy cream

1. Wash and cook the wild rice according to the directions on page 203.

2. While the rice is cooking, sauté the celery and scallions in butter in a medium skillet over medium heat until the celery is crisp-tender, about 5 minutes.

3. In a large mixing bowl, combine all the ingredients except the eggs and cream, and blend well with your hands. Add the eggs and cream and mix again until well blended.

Assembly and Baking
½ cup (1 stick) butter, melted

1. Preheat the oven to 325°F. Divide the stuffing mixture and spread it evenly over each pan, leaving about ¾ inch of the meat uncovered on the long sides and about ¼ inch uncovered on the short ends.

2. Pull up the aluminum foil at one end and begin to roll up the meat and stuffing as you would a jelly roll. Roll up the whole layer; then gently press the ends closed and round them out by patting them. Place the roulades, seam side down, in a greased shallow roasting pan.

3. Cover each roulade with the reserved skin, tucking the ends underneath. Brush the skin with melted butter and bake for 20 minutes per pound, basting occasionally with additional butter.

4. Allow to cool, then refrigerate, covered with aluminum foil, overnight. Reheat in a 325°F. oven for 45 minutes or serve at room temperature.

"When love and skill work together, expect a master-piece."
John Ruskin

144

Old-Fashioned Fresh Cranberry Relish

MAKES ABOUT 3 CUPS

1 medium orange
½ lemon
1 medium apple
3 cups (1 12-ounce package) cranberries
½ cup sugar
¼ teaspoon ground cloves

1. Quarter the orange and lemon and remove the seeds. Quarter the apple and core it. Do not peel the fruit.

2. Grind all the fruit in a food grinder. Stir in the sugar and cloves. Place in a covered nonmetal container (or several small jars) and cover tightly. Refrigerate at least 2 days before serving. This relish keeps for 2 to 3 weeks in the refrigerator.

Puree of Yellow Winter Vegetables

SERVES 18 TO 20

2 pounds carrots
1½ pounds sweet potatoes
1½ pounds yellow turnips (rutabaga)
2 tablespoons salt
6 tablespoons butter, softened
¼ teaspoon grated nutmeg

1. Peel the vegetables and chop them coarsely. Place in a large pot, cover with water, and add the salt. Place over medium-high heat and bring to a boil. Cook until very tender, 15 to 20 minutes.

2. Drain well and then return to the pot. Add the butter and nutmeg and mash with a potato masher until smooth. Beat the mixture with a wooden spoon until fluffy and mound the puree into a large warmed serving bowl.

I've tried making cranberry relish in the food processor, but the texture never came out quite the same as my grandmother's and my mother's relish did. When I asked my mother about it she told me she'd had the same problems trying to use the processor and had gone back to grinding it in a hand food grinder. I guess in some cases there's nothing quite like the sweat of the brow.

Puree of White Winter Vegetables

SERVES 18 TO 20

Here is a wonderful blend of flavors subtly enhanced by the flavor of pears. I like to serve vegetable purees completely unadorned, mounded into large bowls.

1½ pounds turnips
1½ pounds parsnips
1½ pounds celeriac
2 tablespoons salt
2 medium ripe pears
6 tablespoons butter, softened

1. Peel the vegetables and chop them coarsely. Place in a large pot, cover with water, and add the salt. Place over medium-high heat and bring to a boil. Cook until very tender, about 15 minutes.

2. While the vegetables are cooking, peel and core the pears and chop them coarsely. Add the pears to the pot after the vegetables have been cooking for 5 minutes.

3. When the vegetables and pears are tender, drain well and return to the pot. Add the butter and mash with a potato masher until smooth. Beat the mixture with a wooden spoon until fluffy and mound the puree into a large warmed serving bowl.

Marinated Broccoli Salad

SERVES 18 TO 20

4 large bunches broccoli
Juice of 1 lemon
1 cup Red Wine Vinaigrette (page 147)
2 lemons, cut into thin wedges

1. Cut the broccoli into small spears 4 to 5 inches long. In two batches, steam the broccoli in a large pot filled with 1 inch of boiling water and the juice of 1 lemon and fitted with a vegetable steamer. Steam the broccoli until just crisp-tender, about 7 minutes. Remove from the heat and rinse the broccoli with cold water. Drain well.

2. Place the broccoli in a shallow nonmetal pan and pour the vinaigrette over it. Cover and refrigerate at least 3 hours before serving. Toss the broccoli occasionally during marinating time.

3. To serve, remove the broccoli spears from the pan with tongs and arrange in a spoke pattern on a large round serving plate. Arrange the lemon wedges in the center of the plate.

Red Wine Vinaigrette

MAKES ABOUT 1½ CUPS

½ cup red wine vinegar
2 tablespoons Dijon mustard
Salt and freshly ground pepper
1 cup olive oil

In the bowl of a food processor fitted with a metal chopping blade, combine the vinegar, mustard, salt, and pepper to taste. Turn on the processor and add the oil in a slow, steady stream, until a thick, well-blended dressing is achieved. *Or* combine all the ingredients in a bottle or jar, cover, and shake well to combine (this method results in a thinner dressing).

"I will love Christmas in my heart and try to keep it all the year."
Ebenezer Scrooge
A Christmas Carol
by Charles Dickens

Pumpkin-Praline Cheesecake

MAKES ONE 9-INCH CAKE

Even people who don't like pumpkin pie like this creamy cheesecake with its nutty crust, subtly spiced filling, and praline topping. Serve the cake in small slices— it's rich.

Crust
½ cup finely chopped pecans
1 cup graham cracker crumbs
⅓ cup firmly packed light brown sugar
5 tablespoons butter, melted

Filling
3 cups (3 8-ounce packages) cream cheese, softened
¾ cup firmly packed light brown sugar
¾ cup granulated sugar
5 eggs
3 tablespoons all-purpose flour
1 teaspoon ground cinnamon
½ teaspoon ground cloves
½ teaspoon ground ginger
¼ teaspoon grated nutmeg
2 cups pumpkin puree
2 tablespoons Praline *or* Amaretto liqueur
¼ cup heavy cream
½ cup finely chopped pecans

Topping
½ cup sugar
2 tablespoons water
½ cup finely chopped pecans
2 tablespoons light corn syrup

1. Lightly grease a 9-inch springform pan. To make the crust, combine the pecans, graham cracker crumbs, brown sugar, and butter in a mixing bowl and mix well. Press this dough into the bottom and sides of the pan in an even layer and chill for 30 minutes.

2. Preheat the oven to 325°F. To make the filling, cream together the cream cheese and sugars in a large mixing bowl; then beat in the eggs one at a time. Beat the mixture until it is light and somewhat fluffy.

3. In a separate small bowl, stir together the flour and spices with a fork until well blended; then beat this into the cream cheese mixture. Beat in the pumpkin, liqueur, and cream, and then stir in the pecans.

4. Pour the filling mixture into the crust and bake for 1 hour and 45 minutes, or until the top is golden brown. Cool the cake in the pan on a wire rack; then cover with aluminum foil or plastic wrap and refrigerate for at least 3 hours.

5. At least 2 hours before serving, make the praline topping: Combine the sugar and water in a small heavy saucepan and stir over low heat until the sugar has dissolved. Raise the heat and boil rapidly without stirring until the syrup turns a light golden brown, 5 to 7 minutes. Stir in the chopped pecans and pour the mixture out onto a lightly greased baking sheet and cool thoroughly. Chop the cooled praline fine.

6. Remove the sides from the pan and place the cake on a serving dish. Brush the top of the cake lightly with the corn syrup; then sprinkle the chopped praline in an even layer over the cake. Serve the cake cut into very thin wedges.

Cranberry Fool

MAKES ABOUT 6 CUPS

2 cups cranberries
1 cup sugar
2 cups heavy cream

1. Set aside 6 cranberries for garnish; then place the cranberries and sugar in a small heavy saucepan. Place over low heat, and cook, stirring constantly, until all the cranberries pop and a thick syrup has formed. Lightly crush the berries against the side of the pan with the back of the spoon and remove from the heat. Cover and cool; then chill thoroughly.

2. In a chilled bowl, whip the cream until stiff peaks form. Gently fold the cranberry mixture into the whipped cream. Store in the refrigerator, covered, no more than 4 hours before serving.

3. Serve mounded into a glass serving bowl and garnished with the reserved cranberries.

"We have pumpkins at morning, and pumpkins at noon. If it were not for pumpkins, we should be undone."
Anonymous poem, 1630

Pretty pink Cranberry Fool, which makes a nice dessert on its own, spooned into stemmed glasses, is a perfect contrast in color, temperature, and texture to Steamed Ginger Pudding (page 150).

Steamed Ginger Pudding

SERVES 12

This light, golden pudding is a nice alternative to the more traditional and heavier plum pudding. Preserved ginger is available in Oriental and specialty food shops.

2 cups (4 sticks) butter, softened
¼ cup sugar
4 large eggs
5 cups all-purpose flour
2 tablespoons baking powder
½ teaspoon salt
½ teaspoon ground ginger
2 cups milk
1 cup chopped preserved ginger
¾ cup red currant jelly
Cranberry Fool (page 149)

1. In a large mixing bowl, cream together the butter and sugar; then beat in the eggs one at a time.

2. In a separate bowl, sift together the flour, baking powder, salt, and ground ginger; then beat this into the butter-sugar-egg mixture. Slowly beat in the milk and then stir in the preserved ginger.

3. Grease a 2-quart pudding mold, pour in the batter, and put on the lid, or use a turk's head mold covered with aluminum foil. Place the mold in a large kettle and pour hot water into the kettle to come about halfway up the sides of the mold. Cover the kettle, and place over medium heat. Steam the pudding for about 2½ hours, or until a toothpick or cake tester inserted in the center comes out clean. Replenish the hot water as necessary during steaming. (The pudding may be made up to 2 days ahead up to this point and refrigerated.)

4. Allow the pudding to cool for about 1 hour before serving, or if made ahead, bring to room temperature, and then steam for about 45 minutes before serving.

5. To glaze the pudding, melt the red currant preserves in a small heavy saucepan and cook until syrupy, 5 to 7 minutes. Unmold the pudding and invert it onto a serving plate; then brush the glaze onto the pudding, covering the pudding completely. Garnish the plate with sprigs of holly. Serve the warm pudding in thin slices, and top each serving with a generous dollop of Cranberry Fool.

"THE NUTCRACKER'S SWEETS" DESSERT PARTY

•

FOR 20 TO 25

The Nutcracker

•

Tchaikovsky's famous ballet, a favorite at Christmas since George Balanchine introduced it into the repertory of the New York City Ballet in the late 1940s, is not the original incarnation of this magical story, and is in fact only loosely based on the original story, "The Nutcracker and the Mouse King," written by E.T.A. Hoffmann in 1816. The story itself never reached the popularity in America that the ballet has enjoyed, largely because there was never a good translation. In 1984, only one hundred and sixty-eight years after Hoffmann wrote his tale, Maurice Sendak's illustrated version with a new translation became a best-seller.

MENU

Cranberry–Pear Tart

Bûche de Noël with Chestnut–Rum Filling

Chocolate–Almond Torte   Lime Chess Tartlets

Strawberry Mousse in Praline Baskets

Chocolate–Pecan Pie

Champagne Punch with an Ice Wreath

Black and White Fruitcakes (pages 18-21)

Hazelnut Macaroons (page 94)

Homemade Liqueurs (pages 25–27)

A Bowl of Seasonal Fruits

This elegant extravaganza is perhaps the most ambitious menu in this book, but it can also be the most spectacular one. A big bonus is that absolutely everything can be prepared ahead and simply needs to be arranged on a buffet table just before the party begins. Once the table is set with your spectacular array of sweets and the first guest arrives, you're a guest, too.

This menu offers a wide range of tastes, colors, and textures: there's something to satisfy every sweet tooth, whether it craves fruit, nuts, or chocolate, which makes an appearance three times. When you invite your guests, remember to tell them to eat a very light meal beforehand, or even better yet, none at all.

Getting Ready: Since everything is made ahead and there are no courses, the timing need not be so carefully watched here. The Fruitcakes should be made well in advance (see recipes) and the Hazelnut Macaroons can be made up to 2 weeks ahead.

The cake for the Bûche de Noël and the layers for the Chocolate–Almond Torte can be made a day in advance (they can even be frozen in advance, but I prefer not to); the fillings and frostings can be made and the cakes assembled early on the day of the party. The Chocolate–Pecan Pie and Lime Chess Tartlets can also be made a day ahead and refrigerated. You can bake the crust for the Cranberry–Pear Tart and the Praline Baskets the day before, too, but they're best filled on the same day (just remember they both need to chill for 2 hours before serving).

Setting: The attraction here is the beauty and wealth of the offering; let the desserts be the stars. Do garnish the desserts to make them special, and use elaborate serving dishes: footed cake plates, and silver and glass trays and platters. I like to use a lacy white tablecloth on my cherry wood dining table. A huge arrangement of white and pink lilies and early forced peach blossoms in a big clear glass vase makes a simple, dramatic statement. White votive candles in small clear depression glass bowls are set all over the table to heighten the festive mood.

Use salad plates rather than cake plates to serve the desserts so each guest can fit a sampling of several onto his plate. Make sure to have plenty of extra plates and forks on hand so everyone can make a fresh start for seconds.

As far as music goes, I like Vivaldi with desserts (don't ask me why, but they just seem to go well together), and of course, Tchaikovsky's wonderful *Nutcracker*—the whole ballet, not just the suite.

Beverages: In addition to the beverages listed, you can always go for broke and let Champagne flow freely, and also serve espresso or spiced coffee.

Menu Variations: Just about any dessert could be added here, as long as it isn't messy to serve buffet style, and it's elegant rather than "homey." Remember to think in terms of contrasting and complementary flavors, textures, and colors, and to garnish them extravagantly.

Classical Music for Christmas

●

"Christmas Oratorio," Johann Sebastian Bach; "Messiah," George Frederick Handel; "Christmas Symphony," Franz Joseph Haydn; "The Christmas Tree Suite," Franz Liszt; "The Nutcracker," Peter Ilich Tchaikovsky.

Cranberry-Pear Tart

MAKES ONE 10-INCH TART

I like this combination of fruits— the subtle delicacy of the pears balances the hearty tang of the cranberries. Serve the tart in thin slices, garnished with a dollop of sweetened whipped cream or Crème Fraîche (page 131).

¾ cup red currant jelly
¼ cup pear brandy
¼ cup sugar
3 cups (1 12-ounce package) cranberries
1 cup peeled and diced firm ripe pears (2 to 3 pears)
1 tablespoon unflavored gelatin
¼ cup water
1 baked 10-inch tart shell (Pastry Crust, page 47)
1 firm ripe pear, peeled and thinly sliced

1. Place the jelly, brandy, and sugar in a small heavy saucepan and slowly bring to a simmer. Simmer about 10 minutes, then add the cranberries and diced pears and simmer about 5 minutes, or until the cranberries begin to pop. Remove from heat.

2. Soften the gelatin in the water and let stand for 5 minutes. Stir the gelatin into the cranberry mixture until it is dissolved and blended in. Allow the mixture to cool thoroughly.

3. Using a slotted spoon, remove the cranberries and pears from the pan and spread them in an even layer in the baked tart shell.

4. Arrange the pear slices in a fanned-out circle, narrow ends toward the center, in the center of the tart. Allow the cooking liquid to cool to room temperature, then spoon it over the tart, completely covering the fruit. Chill at least 2 hours before serving.

"I said my prayers and ate some cranberry tart for breakfast."

Diary of William Byrd, 1711

Bûche de Noël
with Chestnut-Rum Filling

SERVES 10 TO 12

The French "yule log" cake is traditionally decorated with meringue mushrooms, which I find are more trouble than they're worth unless you've got all the time in the world. The holly decoration described here is prettier and more Christmasy to my eye, not to mention easier. Marzipan holly is generally available at Christmastime, or you can use real holly, or even mint leaves and cranberries to simulate holly. This recipe has a chestnut filling, but two variations are listed below.

Cake
3 large eggs
¾ cup granulated sugar
⅓ cup milk
1 teaspoon vanilla extract
1 cup sifted cake flour
1 teaspoon baking powder
¼ teaspoon salt

Filling
1½ cups canned chestnut puree (*crème de marrons*)
3 tablespoons dark rum
¼ cup confectioners' sugar
½ cup heavy cream

Frosting
6 tablespoons butter
3 ounces unsweetened chocolate
3 cups sifted confectioners' sugar
1½ teaspoons vanilla extract
1 tablespoon dark rum
5 tablespoons milk

Real or marzipan holly

1. Preheat the oven to 375°F. Line a greased 15 × 10-inch jelly roll pan with wax paper; then grease the paper.

2. Beat the eggs in a mixing bowl until light and foamy. Gradually beat in the sugar, and continue beating until the mixture thickens. Beat in the milk and vanilla.

3. In a separate bowl, sift together the flour, baking powder, and salt. Gradually fold the sifted dry ingredients into the liquid mixture.

4. Spread the batter in an even layer in the prepared pan. Bake for 12 minutes, or until the cake is lightly browned and the center springs back when lightly pressed.

5. Loosen the edges of the cake with a knife and invert onto a clean, dry dish or tea towel. Trim the edges of the cake (about ¼ inch) to make straight edges and squared corners. Carefully roll up the cake *and the towel*, starting at the 10-inch end. Place the rolled cake, seam side down, on a wire rack to cool.

6. To make the filling, blend together the chestnut puree, rum, and sugar in a small mixing bowl. In a separate chilled bowl, whip the cream until stiff peaks form. Fold the whipped cream into the chestnut mixture. Refrigerate until needed.

7. To make the frosting, melt the butter and chocolate together in a small heavy saucepan over low heat, stirring constantly. Combine the sugar, vanilla, rum, and milk in a medium mixing bowl. Slowly add the melted chocolate and butter to the mixing bowl until well combined and the frosting is smooth. Set aside.

8. To assemble, carefully unroll the cooled cake and remove the towel. Spread the cake evenly with the filling, reserving about ¾ cup. Reroll the cake and place it, seam side down, on an oval or rectangular serving platter, a bit closer to one end of the platter.

9. Frost all but the ends of the cake, reserving about ¼ cup of the frosting. Spread the frosting on with long strokes from one end to the other, simulating bark.

10. Using a wet knife, cut off a 1-inch slice from the end closest to the end of the platter. Gently press the slice, cut side up, onto the side of the "trunk," to simulate a sawed-off branch.

11. Mix ¼ cup of the reserved filling with the reserved frosting. Cover the two ends of the log and the end of the sawed-off branch with the remaining filling. Swirl spirals of the combined frosting and filling mixture onto the three ends to simulate the rings of a sawed off tree.

12. Decorate with a few real or marzipan holly sprigs. Refrigerate the cake until serving time.

Raspberry Cream Filling Substitute strained raspberry jam for the chestnut puree and framboise liqueur for the rum.

Mocha Cream Filling Substitute fudge sauce for the chestnut puree and coffee liqueur (such as Kahlua) for the rum.

Chocolate-Almond Torte

MAKES ONE 9-INCH CAKE

This cake is my idea of heaven: raspberry-glazed almond layers with chocolate buttercream in between and a chocolate glaze overall. And it's a beauty, all dark and shiny with a chocolate raspberry "poinsettia" as the crowning glory. This is somewhat complicated, but it's not difficult, and believe me, it's worth every second in the kitchen. If you're going to go through all this work, do spring for the raspberries for the center of the "poinsettia." You only need a few, but the rest won't go to waste—they make a great snack for the baker.

10 large eggs
1 cup sugar
¼ teaspoon salt
½ teaspoon vanilla extract
½ teaspoon almond extract
¾ cup fine dry bread crumbs
2 cups ground almonds
Pinch of cream of tartar
⅔ cup raspberry jam
2 tablespoons framboise *or* vodka
Chocolate Buttercream (recipe follows)
Chocolate Glaze (page 190)
6 Chocolate Leaves (page 190)
5 fresh raspberries *or* whole hazelnuts

1. Preheat the oven to 350°F. Grease two 9-inch layer pans very well, line with wax paper; then grease the paper.

2. Separate the eggs into two large mixing bowls. Add ¾ cup sugar, salt, and vanilla and almond extracts to the bowl containing the yolks. Beat until foamy and thickened. Stir in the bread crumbs and ground nuts.

3. Add a pinch of cream of tartar to the egg whites and beat until they form soft peaks. Gradually add the remaining ¼ cup sugar, beating until it is incorporated into the whites and stiff peaks form.

4. Fold about a third of the egg white mixture into the egg yolk mixture; then gently fold this mixture back into the remaining egg whites.

5. Divide the batter between the two prepared cake pans. Bake about 45 minutes, or until the surface of the layers is firm to the touch and the layers are lightly browned.

6. Turn the layers out onto wire racks, and gently peel off the wax paper; then invert the layers again so they are top side up.

7. In a small heavy saucepan, combine the raspberry jam and the framboise or vodka. Heat slowly to a spreadable consistency; then strain.

8. Spread half of the jam glaze onto each of the cooling layers; then allow the layers to cool completely.

9. Place one layer on an aluminum foil–covered 9-inch circle of cardboard. Spread the chocolate buttercream evenly across this layer, reserving about ¼ cup. Place the other layer onto the bottom layer and smooth out the space between the layers with the reserved buttercream. Cover the torte with aluminum foil and refrigerate for 1 hour, or until the buttercream is firm. (May be made and chilled for up to 24 hours at this point.) While the torte is chilling, make the Chocolate Glaze.

10. Place the torte, on its cardboard circle, on a wire rack. Pour most of the glaze over the cake. Tilt the cake from side to side to evenly coat the top and sides. Patch any bare spots with the remaining glaze, if necessary. You must work quickly glazing the torte.

11. Allow the glaze to cool and place the torte on a serving plate. Arrange the chocolate leaves in a circle, pointed ends facing out, in the center of the torte, to simulate a poinsettia. Mound the raspberries in the center of the flower. Store the torte in the refrigerator.

Chocolate Buttercream
1 large egg yolk
1 tablespoon chocolate liqueur
3 tablespoons sugar
1½ ounces unsweetened chocolate
½ teaspoon vanilla extract
¼ cup (½ stick) butter, softened
¼ cup heavy cream

1. Combine the egg yolk and liqueur in a small mixing bowl and beat until thickened. Add the sugar, 1 tablespoon at a time, beating continuously until foamy.

2. Melt the chocolate in the top of a double boiler over simmering water; then remove the double boiler from heat.

3. Gradually stir in the egg mixture until well blended. Place the double boiler back over low heat and cook about 2 minutes, or until the mixture thickens (do not allow to simmer). Stir in vanilla and remove from heat. Allow to cool slightly.

4. In a medium mixing bowl, beat the butter; then gradually beat in the egg-chocolate mixture.

> **"If you aren't up to a little magic occasionally, you shouldn't waste time trying to cook."**
> *Colette*

5. In a separate small chilled bowl, whip the cream until stiff peaks form. Fold the whipped cream gently into the egg-chocolate-butter mixture until just blended.

Chocolate Glaze
12 ounces semisweet chocolate
1½ cups heavy cream

1. Melt the chocolate and cream together in the top of a double boiler over simmering water. Stirring constantly, bring the mixture to a simmer. Immediately remove from heat.

2. Let mixture cool to a lukewarm temperature. (Do not allow to cool to room temperature or the glaze will become too thick.) Immediately pour onto the torte (see above).

Chocolate Leaves
Melt 1 to 2 ounces semisweet chocolate and paint the chocolate onto the backs of washed and dried lemon or camellia leaves (available from florists) with a clean narrow pastry brush. Place the leaves on aluminum foil, coated sides up, and allow to cool; then chill. When the chocolate has hardened, gently and carefully peel the leaves away from the chocolate from the stem end. Handle the chocolate leaves carefully to avoid getting fingerprints on the surface.

Lime Chess Tartlets

MAKES 3 DOZEN 2-INCH TARTLETS

2 recipes Pastry Crust (see page 47)
2 cups sugar
6 large eggs, well beaten
5 teaspoons cornmeal
½ cup (1 stick) butter, melted
Juice and grated rind of 3 limes
Grated rind of 2 limes

1. Preheat the oven to 350°F. Roll out the Pastry Crust and line tartlet tins. Prebake the tartlet shells for 10 minutes; then remove them from the oven.

*S*outherners are known for their sweet tooths, and these tangy tartlets satisfy that craving without being too heavy at the end of a big meal, or as part of a dessert buffet. These can be made a day ahead and refrigerated.

2. Blend the sugar and eggs, beating until smooth; then add the cornmeal. Stir in the melted butter, lime juice, and grated rinds of 3 limes. Blend until smooth.

3. Fill the tart shells with the mixture until not quite full. Sprinkle the surface of the tartlets with the remaining grated rinds. Bake for 20 minutes, or until the surface is a light golden color.

4. Remove from the oven and place on wire racks to cool. Store, loosely covered, in the refrigerator. Just before serving, sprinkle grated lime rind onto the tarlets.

Strawberry Mousse in Praline Baskets

MAKES ABOUT 4 DOZEN

3 cups strawberries
3 tablespoons unflavored gelatin
½ cup sugar
4 large egg whites
2 cups heavy cream
½ recipe Praline Baskets (page 198)
About 24 strawberries, halved

1. Puree the berries in a food processor fitted with a steel chopping blade; then transfer the puree to a heavy saucepan and stir in the gelatin and half of the sugar. Place over low heat and stir constantly until the sugar and gelatin have dissolved.

2. Transfer the mixture to a mixing bowl and place the bowl over ice water. Stir the mixture until it starts to thicken, about 5 minutes.

3. In a separate bowl, beat the egg whites until soft peaks form; then beat in the remaining sugar.

4. In a third chilled bowl, whip the cream until stiff peaks form. Fold the whipped cream into the berry mixture; then fold in the egg white mixture until all is just blended.

5. Using a pastry bag fitted with a small star tip, pipe the mousse into the Praline Baskets and garnish each with a strawberry half. Chill at least 2 hours before serving.

*T*hese are wonderful not only as part of a buffet but as an accompaniment to espresso as a light finish to a big dinner.

Chocolate-Pecan Pie

MAKES ONE 10-INCH PIE

Some dyed-in-the-wool Southerners might balk at the idea of adding chocolate to their beloved pecan pie, but this is a sure 'nough authentic recipe from the kitchen of Evelyn Spainhour of Winston-Salem, North Carolina. All right, I'll admit it—I'm the one who added the booze. Try this pie with walnuts, too.

1⅓ cups semisweet chocolate chips
4 large eggs
⅔ cup sugar
1¼ cups light corn syrup
¼ cup dark rum
1 teaspoon vanilla extract
1½ cups pecan halves
1 unbaked 10-inch Pastry Crust (page 47)

1. Preheat the oven to 375°F.

2. Melt the chocolate over low heat in a small heavy saucepan or in the top of a double boiler over simmering water. Remove from heat and allow to cool slightly.

3. Break the eggs into a mixing bowl and beat lightly. Beat in the sugar, corn syrup, rum, and vanilla. Gradually beat in the cooled melted chocolate until all is well blended; then stir in 1 cup pecans.

4. Pour the mixture into the unbaked pie shell and arrange the remaining pecans on top. Bake for 45 minutes, or until the filling is set and the edges of the pie shell are golden brown.

5. Remove to a wire rack to cool. Serve either slightly warm or chilled with sweetened whipped cream (or a small scoop of vanilla ice cream if you want to be truly decadent).

Note: Use leftover pastry scraps to make decorative leaves. Brush the edges of the unbaked filled pie shell with water and apply the decorations (see photograph on pages 170–171).

Champagne Punch with an Ice Wreath

MAKES 50 SERVINGS

2 pints apricot brandy
1 bottle Sauternes
2 liters ginger ale
3 magnums or 6 bottles dry Champagne

1. Chill all the individual ingredients thoroughly several hours before serving.

2. Just before serving, stir the brandy and Sauternes together in a large punch bowl until well blended. Gently stir in the ginger ale and Champagne. Carefully place the unmolded and inverted ice wreath in the bowl.

Ice Wreath
5 kiwis
5 limes
10 strawberries, hulled

1. Peel the kiwis and cut them in half lengthwise; then cut the halves into thin, half-round slices. Cut the limes into thin, half-round slices. Halve the strawberries.

2. Arrange the strawberries, evenly spaced, in the bottom of a 4-cup ring mold. Spread the kiwi and lime slices on top of the berries and up the sides of the mold. Carefully, fill the mold with cold water and freeze until solid.

"I was enjoying myself now I had taken two finger bowls of Champagne, and the scene had changed before my eyes into something significant, elemental, and profound."
F. Scott Fitzgerald

"THE TWELVE DAYS OF CHRISTMAS" WEEKNIGHT DINNER

•

FOR 6 TO 8

MENU

Smoked Salmon with Horseradish–Mustard Cream

Simple Broiled Duckling

Cranberry–Kumquat Compote

Warm Cajun Brussels Sprouts Salad

Mimi's Potato Latkes

Pumpkin–Black Walnut Cake

*T*his dinner doesn't have anything to do with the items listed in the song, but it can be served during the twelve days of Christmas (or any other time for that matter) and is especially good on a night when you don't want to spend a whole lot of time in the kitchen.

This is the same menu I served to a group of friends about six years ago during the holidays. The wine flowed freely, and sometime between the main course and dessert my friend Lindsay

"The most essential thing for happiness is the gift of friendship."

Sir William Osler

Miller decided everyone should know all the hand motions for "The Twelve Days of Christmas" that she had learned as a girl. Soon eight otherwise normal adults were singing at the tops of our lungs and impersonating everything from twelve drummers drumming to a partridge in a pear tree. This new tradition has been repeated by the same group every year since. While the menu itself has nothing to do with the lyrics of the song, to me this dinner has very much to do with the spirit of the song and the season, friends of different backgrounds and faiths sharing warmth, happiness, and good food.

Getting Ready: For this dinner, you need to be in the kitchen for about 45 minutes off and on just before dinnertime, but that's about it. Arrange the smoked salmon and sauce first, which only takes a few minutes. The duck, which should be marinated for at least one day, takes about 45 minutes to broil. The Potato Latkes need to be made at the last minute or they become soggy.

The Cranberry–Kumquat Compote can be made up to a week in advance, and the Brussels sprouts can be steamed and marinated up to a day ahead. Warm the salad and toss in the pecans just before serving. The Pumpkin–Black Walnut Cake can be made several days in advance.

Beverages: With the first course, serve iced vodka with sprigs of dill, or a Sauvignon Blanc. For the main course, try a red Burgundy or a Pinot Noir, and after dessert homemade Irish Cream Liqueur (page 26) makes for a nice finish.

Setting: Since it's a "school night," don't go overboard with the table setting, but do remember that an attractive table always makes a meal taste better. I set the table very simply without a tablecloth, using gold-rimmed white dinner plates set on brass service plates, simple silver, "everyday" wineglasses, and white damask napkins. An easily put together but spectacular center-piece is created by filling a twig basket with pine cones, wisps of evergreen, small colorful fruits, and a half dozen white candles.

Menu Variations: Onion–Rosemary Tartlets (page 72) would make a nice appetizer alternative, as would Smoked Salmon Mousse (page 189). For a lighter dessert you might try Spiced Apple-Ginger Sorbet (page 169).

Smoked Salmon with Horseradish-Mustard Cream

SERVES 8

This first course can be served from a large platter in the living room before sitting down at the table, or serve it on individual plates in the dining room.

1 cup heavy cream
¼ cup prepared horseradish
2 teaspoons Dijon mustard
2 teaspoons lemon juice
¼ teaspoon salt
⅛ teaspoon cayenne pepper
12 thin slices dark pumpernickel bread
1 pound thinly sliced smoked salmon
2 to 3 tablespoons snipped chives

1. In a chilled mixing bowl, whip the cream until stiff peaks form. In a separate bowl, combine the horseradish, mustard, lemon juice, salt, and pepper; then fold this mixture into the whipped cream.

2. Trim the crusts from the bread and cut each slice into triangled quarters. Arrange the bread around the edge of a platter or individual serving plates, then arrange the sliced smoked salmon in the center of the platter or plates. Place a chilled bowl of horseradish–mustard cream at one end of the platter or generous dollops of the cream on the individual plates and sprinkle the snipped chives over the cream.

"Christmas is a time for me to be a heavenly host as well as the birthday boy."
Noel Coward

Simple Broiled Duckling

SERVES 8

*D*uck has become more and more readily available, but it's still not served often enough as far as I'm concerned. Duck can be cooked in many ways, but I prefer this simple method of marinating it then broiling it quickly. Use corrugated aluminum foil broiling pans for a quick cleanup, but be careful in handling them so as not to spill any hot fat. The wings aren't used here but they make an excellent addition to a stockpot.

4 medium shallots, minced
4 bay leaves, coarsely crushed
10 garlic cloves, finely chopped
1 tablespoon coarse salt
1 tablespoon black peppercorns, crushed
2 teaspoons dried thyme
2 cups dry red wine
4 4- to 5-pound ducklings, wings removed, and quartered

1. Combine all the ingredients except the ducks in a large jar. Cover and shake well. Set aside.

2. Trim the ducks of all excess fat and prick the skins all over with a fork. Dump the ducks into a strong, clean plastic bag. Pour the marinade into the bag, shake the bag about to coat the ducks all over, and then tie the bag shut. Refrigerate at least overnight; 2 days is better. Shake the bag occasionally to distribute the marinade.

3. To broil, remove the ducks from the refrigerator an hour ahead of time and allow them to come to room temperature. Preheat the broiler for about 10 minutes.

4. Remove the ducks from the bag and discard the bag and marinade. Wipe the ducks with paper towels to remove the moisture. Arrange the duck quarters skin side down on two aluminum foil broiling pans and place on a rack 4 to 5 inches below the heat source. Broil for 10 minutes.

5. Remove the pans from the broiler and carefully pour off the fat. Turn the ducks over with tongs and prick the skin again to release the excess fat. Return the pans to the broiler and broil for 20 to 25 minutes, or until the skin is crisp and well browned, and the juices are only slightly tinged with pink when the meat is pierced with a knife. (This is for medium-rare duck, the way I like it; cook about 5 minutes longer for medium-well.)

6. To serve, arrange 2 duck quarters on individual dinner plates, spoon some Cranberry–Kumquat Compote (recipe follows) onto each serving, and garnish with curls of orange zest.

Cranberry-Kumquat Compote

MAKES ABOUT 3 CUPS

½ pound kumquats
½ cup dry red wine
¾ cup sugar
½ teaspoon ground ginger
3 cups (1 12-ounce package) cranberries
Curls of orange zest

1. Slice the kumquats in half lengthwise and place in a medium heavy saucepan with the red wine, sugar, and ginger. Cook over medium heat until the mixture begins to simmer.

2. Add the cranberries and simmer for about 10 minutes, or until the cranberries begin to pop and the liquid in the pan becomes somewhat syrupy. Remove from heat, cool, cover, and chill until needed.

3. Serve with Simple Broiled Duckling or in a small chilled serving bowl, garnished with curls of orange zest.

Cajun Brussels Sprouts Salad

SERVES 6 TO 8

¼ cup olive oil
¼ cup peanut oil
⅓ cup tarragon vinegar
2 garlic cloves, very finely chopped
1 tablespoon chopped parsley
¼ teaspoon dried basil
Pinch salt, or to taste
Pinch cayenne pepper, or to taste
1 small red onion, coarsely chopped
2 10-ounce containers Brussels sprouts
½ cup coarsely chopped pecans

1. Combine all the ingredients except the Brussels sprouts and pecans in a screwtop jar, cover, and shake well. Set aside.

*K*umquats are small oval citrus fruits often used for decoration, but here they are put to better use in a perfect marriage with cranberries. This simple compote goes very well with both the duck and the potato latkes in this menu, and is also a nice accompaniment to pork, turkey, and ham.

*M*y friend Dana Landry brought this recipe with him when he moved up North from New Orleans. Served warm or at room temperature, this salad is a nice alternative as a vegetable side dish.

2. Wash the Brussels sprouts well, and remove any tough or yellowed outer leaves. Slice the sprouts in half and steam in a vegetable steamer for about 5 minutes, or until crisp-tender and a vivid green. Remove the sprouts to a bowl, pour the dressing over them, cover, and chill for 2 to 3 hours.

3. Bring the salad to room temperature before serving or warm it in a heavy pan over very low heat. Add the chopped pecans just before serving and toss well to combine.

Mimi's Potato Latkes

SERVES 8

4 large baking potatoes
2 medium onions
2 large eggs, lightly beaten
2 tablespoons matzoh meal *or* all-purpose flour
¼ teaspoon salt
¼ teaspoon freshly ground black pepper
Vegetable or corn oil for frying

1. Peel the potatoes and onions and grate them, using a hand grater or food processor fitted with a steel grating blade. Place the mixture in a colander and squeeze out the excess liquid.

2. Combine the grated mixture with the eggs and matzoh meal and season with salt and pepper. Stir to blend well. The batter should be the consistency of thick cream.

3. Pour enough oil into a large skillet to cover the surface and place over medium heat until sizzling. Drop the batter by heaping tablespoonfuls about ¼ inch thick into the skillet and flatten with the back of the spoon. Cook about 5 minutes, or until the bottoms are golden brown. Turn the pancakes over and cook the other sides until browned, about 3 minutes. Place the finished pancakes into a paper towel–lined pan in a slow oven and repeat the frying process until the batter is used up. Serve immediately.

Latkes (potato pancakes) are a traditional Hanukkah food and very much a part of the holiday season. In addition to being served as a side dish, Mimi Benowitz's famous latkes are wonderful for breakfast or lunch, served with applesauce or sour cream. These should be made just before serving or they lose their crisp texture. If you must make them ahead, reheat them on a baking sheet in a 350° F. oven for about 20 minutes.

Pumpkin-Black Walnut Cake

MAKES ONE 9-INCH, 2-LAYER CAKE

This cake is dense, rich, and decadent. If you dare, top a slice with a scoop of maple-walnut ice cream. This cake keeps quite well for 4 to 5 days, but it seldom lasts that long.

1½ cups coarsely chopped black walnuts
2 cups all-purpose flour
1½ teaspoons baking powder
1½ teaspoons baking soda
¾ teaspoon salt
1½ teaspoons ground cinnamon
1½ teaspoons ground ginger
1½ teaspoons ground cloves
1 teaspoon grated nutmeg
2 cups sugar
¾ cup vegetable oil
4 large eggs, lightly beaten
1½ cups (fresh or canned) pumpkin puree
½ teaspoon vanilla extract
Sour Cream Frosting *or* Cream Cheese–Nut Frosting (page 217)

"THE TWELVE DAYS OF CHRISTMAS" DINNER is perfect for weeknight entertaining with its easily assembled fruit and evergreen centerpiece and easy-to-make main course: Simple Broiled Duckling with Cranberry-Kumquat Compote; Mimi's Potato Latkes; and Warm Cajun Brussels Sprouts Salad.

1. Preheat the oven to 350°F. Grease two 9-inch round cake pans, line with wax paper, and grease the paper.

2. Spread the chopped black walnuts out on a baking sheet and toast lightly in the oven, about 10 minutes. Set aside.

3. In a large mixing bowl, sift together the flour, baking powder, baking soda, salt, and spices; then stir in the sugar. Beat in the oil, eggs, pumpkin puree, and vanilla; then fold in 1 cup of the toasted walnuts.

4. Divide the batter between the prepared pans and place on the middle rack of the oven. Bake for 40 to 45 minutes, or until the edges of the cakes begin to pull away from the sides of the pans and a cake tester inserted in the center comes out clean.

5. Remove the pans from the oven, turn the layers out onto wire racks, and peel off the wax paper; then cool. When the layers are completely cool, place one layer on a serving plate and frost the top with about a quarter of the Sour Cream Frosting. Place the second layer onto the iced one and frost the top and side of the cake. Sprinkle the remaining walnuts over the top of the cake.

"THE NUTCRACKER'S SWEETS" DESSERT PARTY during Christmas week—what could be more fun than a celebration of sweet indulgence (clockwise from center): Cranberry-Pear Tart; Buche de Noël with Chestnut-Rum Filling; Chocolate-Almond Torte; Champagne Punch; Hazelnut Macaroons, Strawberry Mousse in Praline Baskets, and Lime Chess Tartlets; Black Bourbon Fruitcake and Martha Washington's White Fruitcake; and Chocolate Pecan Pie.

A CHAMPAGNE PARTY on New Year's Eve rings in the new year with an eclectic spread of hors d'oeuvres laid out against a backdrop of splendid opulence (clockwise from center): Smoked Salmon Mousse with Cucumber Slices; Red Pepper Cheese with starshaped Melba Toasts; Raw Vegetables with Curried Cream; Caviar Stuffed Eggs; Aubergine Caviar with Endive; Chocolate-Praline Lace Cookies; Banana-Nut Cakes; Prairie Caviar with Tortilla Chips; Veal and Ham Pâté; Strawberries with Pistachio Cream; and Fruit Wrapped in Smoked Turkey and Prosciutto.

"THE MORNING-AFTER" BUFFET BRUNCH starts the new year off brightly with kitchen kitsch, a basket of daisies, and comforting foods (clockwise from bottom right): Ham and Cheese in Puff Pastry; Confetti Home Fries; Grandma Wynn's Sautéed Apples; Faye's Coffee Cake; warm Orange Gingerbread; and Screwdrivers and Bloodies.

A ROMANTIC CANDLELIGHT DINNER for you and that certain someone on New Year's Eve. What could be more romantic than a roaring fire, flickering candles, fragrant roses, bubbly Champagne, and a sumptuous meal? The main course offers Rack of Lamb with a Coat of Many Colors; Wild Rice with Morels; Sautéed Cherry Tomatoes; and a Green Salad with Red Pepper Hearts and Champagne Vinaigrette.

A FIRESIDE TEA PARTY

•

FOR 6

A FIRESIDE TEA PARTY promises a few hours of peace and relaxation during Christmas week. Floral china, pink Depression glass, antique silver, and old lace set a luxurious stage for a cozy afternoon. The menu features a tasty array (clockwise from bottom): star and heart-shaped Tea Scones with cranberries; Chocolate-Banana Bread; Lemon Curd and Quick Homemade Jam; Lemon Velvet Tea Cake; Chocolate-Liqueur Dipped Strawberries; Angelic Cream Puffs; and Tea Sandwiches.

*T*eatime. The very idea conjures up images of a few stolen hours, a moment in the late afternoon when you can light a fire, take off your shoes, indulge in a few comforting delicacies, and forget everyday affairs. If there were ever a referendum to make teatime an everyday national observance, I would support it wholeheartedly, because teatime lets us escape from a hectic world of pressures and be good to ourselves.

I was first introduced to "high tea" at the Connaught Hotel in London, where I sat back in an overstuffed wing chair after a long day of shopping. When the tea service was presented, little did I know that a proper pot of tea is accompanied by another pot of hot water so that each imbiber may mix the tea to his own desired strength. Foolish American, me—I proceeded to pour myself a cupful of hot water and then asked the waiter for a tea bag! My *faux pas* was graciously overlooked and my teacup hastily replaced and filled for me. As I sipped my perfectly brewed tea, a gleaming tea cart laden with wonderful, tiny sandwiches was brought before me for my selection, soon followed by another cart bearing a mouth-watering array of sweets. Ah, civilization!

This menu offers a variety of treats, all of which can be made ahead so the host can be a pampered guest, too. With the atmosphere relaxed and cozy and the conversation bright, a holiday tea party is one of the best gifts we can give to ourselves.

Getting Ready: The Lemon Velvet Tea Cake and Chocolate–Banana Bread can be made up to a week ahead, or made well in advance and frozen, tightly wrapped. The Lemon Curd is from Making Things Ahead (page 14). The cream puffs can be made and filled early in the day, covered, and refrigerated, as can the two kinds of sandwiches (don't make any of these too far in advance or they become soggy). The tea scones are best made on the same day. Dip the fruits in chocolate early in the day or even the day before. The only thing you have to make at serving time is the tea itself, but that's a leisurely pleasure.

Setting: Here's the opportunity to use everything you own that's at all fussy. I like to arrange my silver tea service and prettiest china teacups, saucers, and small plates on a lace-covered tea table, alongside a white porcelain vase filled with an extravagant bouquet of mixed pink and white flowers. On the lower coffee table, I set out the food, arranged on silver, china, and pink depression glass serving dishes. To enhance the mood I like to put on recordings of Gershwin, Porter, and Coward; then after lighting the fireplace, I'm in business! (If you don't have a fireplace, elaborate crystal or silver candelabra fitted with long white tapers and placed on the tables will add a cozy glow.)

Beverages: Hints for brewing the perfect pot of tea are included with the recipes. If you want to serve an alcoholic beverage, you can never go wrong with sherry or champagne, followed by any of the homemade liqueurs (pages 25–27) to accompany the sweets.

Menu Variations: This menu has more than enough to satisfy six people—you may want to eliminate one of the sweets—but I like to have a rather abundant array of goodies for my guests to choose from. Almost any dessert, as long as it's truly an indulgence, would go well here. Hot Popovers (page 106) are another teatime delight, but they do have to be baked just before serving.

"There are few hours in life more agreeable than the hours dedicated to the ceremony known as afternoon tea."
Henry James

Cucumber and Radish Sandwiches

MAKES 12 TEA-SIZE SANDWICHES

---

1 cucumber, peeled, seeded, and thinly sliced
2 tablespoons mayonnaise
¼ teaspoon salt
¼ cup (½ stick) butter, softened
3 tablespoons chopped chives
6 thin slices firm white bread, crusts removed
8 radishes, thinly sliced

1. Place the cucumbers, mayonnaise, and salt in a small bowl and toss to coat the cucumbers. Cover and place in the refrigerator to marinate for 1 hour. Remove from the refrigerator and drain the cucumbers.

2. Combine the butter and chives in a small bowl and blend thoroughly with a fork.

3. Spread the chive butter evenly in a thin layer onto the bread. Layer three slices of the bread with the drained cucumber; then add a layer of sliced radishes. Top with the other three slices, buttered side down, and press gently to adhere. Reserve remaining cucumber and radish slices for garnish.

4. With a sharp knife, diagonally cut each sandwich into quarters, making four triangular sandwiches. Stack the sandwiches and cover tightly with aluminum foil or plastic wrap. Refrigerate until serving time.

5. To serve, garnish with cucumber slices and radish slices. Arrange the sandwiches on a pretty china plate with a few fresh flowers.

Brewing the Perfect Pot of Tea

●

Put a tea kettle of cold water onto the stove over high heat. While waiting for the water to heat up, warm the teapot by filling it with hot tap water, and letting it stand for a few minutes. Pour out the water before using.

Fill a tea ball with tea leaves, allowing 1 teaspoon tea leaves for each cup of water. Place the tea ball in the bottom of the teapot. Pour the boiling water into the teapot. Put the cover on the teapot and cover the pot with a tea cozy or heavy cloth to keep it warm. Steep the tea about 5 minutes.

Serve the tea with an additional pot of hot water, for guests who prefer the tea weaker. Serve the tea with milk, honey, sugar, and lemon wedges.

When brewing tea, you may want to add any of the following to the tea ball: dried lemon or orange peel, whole allspice or cloves, or dried mint leaves. A few cinnamon sticks could be added to the pot also.

Bacon, Horseradish, and Tomato Sandwiches

MAKES 12 TEA-SIZE SANDWICHES

¼ pound bacon, coarsely chopped
¼ cup (½ stick) butter, softened
4 teaspoons prepared horseradish
6 thin slices dark pumpernickel bread, crusts removed
2 medium ripe tomatoes, seeded and thinly sliced

1. In a small skillet, sauté the bacon until brown and crisp. Drain and cool on paper towels; reserve the bacon fat for another use. Crumble the bacon well.

2. Combine the butter, crumbled bacon, and horseradish in a small mixing bowl and blend thoroughly with a fork.

3. Spread the butter mixture evenly in a thin layer onto the bread. Layer three slices of the bread with a single layer of tomato; then top with the other three slices, buttered side down. Press gently to make the sandwiches adhere.

4. With a sharp knife, cut each sandwich into quarters, to make four long finger sandwiches. Stack the sandwiches and cover tightly with aluminum foil or plastic wrap. Refrigerate until serving time.

Note: If good-quality tomatoes are unavailable, substitute strips of roasted red peppers (see page 90).

"The things we do at Christmas are touched with a certain extravagance, as beautiful, in some aspects, as the extravagance of Nature in June."
Robert Collyer

Tea Scones

MAKES 1 DOZEN

Scones, a traditional tea bread from the British Isles, have recently become quite popular in the United States as a breakfast bread. These scones are smaller and lighter than the commercial ones most often found in America, and they don't toughen when cooled to room temperature. Many Englishmen consider scones to be the perfect excuse for consuming extravagant amounts of jam and clotted cream. Alas, clotted cream is not readily available in this country, but Lemon Curd (page 17) is a delicious alternative, lavishly spread onto split scones.

2 cups sifted all-purpose flour
2 tablespoons sugar
¼ teaspoon salt
2½ teaspoons baking powder
¼ cup (½ stick) cold butter
2 large eggs
½ cup heavy cream

1. Preheat the oven to 400°F. Grease a large baking sheet well.

2. Sift together the flour, sugar, salt, and baking powder in a medium mixing bowl, or the bowl of a food processor fitted with a metal chopping blade.

3. Cut in the butter, using a pastry blender, if mixing in a bowl, or by processing with a quick pulsing action, if using the processor.

4. In a separate small bowl, beat together the eggs and cream. Reserve 2 tablespoons of this mixture; then pour into the flour-butter mixture. Mix together until just blended (do not use the food processor for this step, as the dough will become overblended.

5. With floured hands, pat the dough out onto a floured board into a layer ½-inch-thick and approximately 9 inches square (do not use a rolling pin). Using a floured knife, cut the dough into approximate 3-inch squares; then cut each square in half on the diagonal. *Or* use heart-shaped and star-shaped cookie cutters to shape the scones.

6. Carefully place the scones on the prepared baking sheet and brush the reserved egg-cream mixture lightly over the surface to glaze. Bake for 10 to 12 minutes, or until risen and golden brown. Serve immediately, or cool on a rack and serve at room temperature.

Variations One-half cup of any of the following during the final mixing at the end of step 4: dried currants soaked in 3 tablespoons cassis; a mixture of candied orange peel and candied ginger; chopped apples mixed with 2 tablespoons crumbled Stilton cheese; a mixture of chopped dates and walnuts; a mixture of chopped cranberries and pecans. Also try adding ½ teaspoon grated lemon or orange rind.

Chocolate-Banana Bread

MAKES ONE 9×5×3-INCH LOAF
OR TWO 8×3×2½-INCH LOAVES

This bread combines two of my food passions, bananas and chocolate. The recipe came from my Aunt Florence, who loved having afternoon bridge parties, where she served this bread with tea. I use the food processor to make the batter so the bananas are blended in well.

½ cup (1 stick) butter, at room temperature
1 cup sugar
2 large eggs
1½ cups all-purpose flour
2 teaspoons baking powder
¼ teaspoon baking soda
½ teaspoon salt
1 teaspoon ground cinnamon
1½ cups mashed very ripe banana
1 teaspoon vanilla extract
3 ounces semisweet chocolate, coarsely grated
¾ cup coarsely chopped walnuts

1. Preheat the oven to 350°F. Grease one 9 × 5 × 3-inch or two 8 × 3 × 2½-inch loaf pans.

2. In the bowl of a food processor fitted with the steel chopping blade, cream the butter and sugar together, then add the eggs and mix well.

3. In a separate mixing bowl, sift together the flour, baking powder, baking soda, salt, and cinnamon. Add this mixture to the food processor bowl and process to blend well. Add the bananas and vanilla and blend in.

4. Using a large spoon, stir (do not process) in the chocolate and walnuts.

5. Pour the batter into the prepared pan(s) and bake for 1 hour and 10 minutes, or until a toothpick inserted into the bread comes out clean. Remove the bread from the pan and cool on wire racks. Store, tightly wrapped in plastic wrap or aluminum foil, at room temperature up to 3 days.

Lemon Velvet Tea Cake

MAKES ONE 10-INCH TUBE CAKE,
12 TO 16 SERVINGS

This heavenly cake is delicious served with a hot cup of tea. In the summertime, serve it topped with pureed raspberries.

1 cup (2 sticks) butter, softened
4 ounces cream cheese, softened
1¾ cups sugar
3 large eggs
1 tablespoon grated lemon rind
1½ cups all-purpose flour
1 teaspoon baking powder
Confectioners' sugar

1. Preheat the oven to 375°F. Grease a flat-bottomed 10-inch tube pan very well, line the bottom with wax paper, and grease the paper.

2. In a large mixing bowl, beat together the butter and cream cheese until well blended; then beat in the sugar, eggs, and lemon rind and beat until the mixture is light and fluffy. In a separate bowl, sift together the flour and baking powder; then beat this into the butter mixture.

3. Spoon the batter into the prepared pan and bake for 55 to 60 minutes, or until the cake is a light golden brown and springs back firmly when pressed lightly. Cool for 15 minutes in the pan; then invert onto a wire rack to cool completely.

4. Place the cake upside down on a work surface. Center a round paper doily on the cake and carefully sprinkle with confectioners' sugar, holding the doily down against the cake with your other hand. Remove to a cake plate to serve.

Glazed Lemon Tea Cake Use a Bundt pan rather than a tube pan, and grease the pan very well. Do not dust with confectioners' sugar, but rather drizzle on a glaze made by combining ½ cup confectioners' sugar with 1 tablespoon lemon juice.

Angelic Cream Puffs

MAKES ABOUT 24 MINIATURE PUFFS

These little morsels are truly melt-in-the-mouth. Do try some of the variations of the basic pastry cream.

½ cup (1 stick) butter
1 cup water
1 cup all-purpose flour
4 large eggs
Pasty Cream (recipe follows)
Confectioners' sugar *or* curls of orange rind

1. Preheat the oven to 400°F. Grease a baking sheet well.

2. Combine the butter and water in a heavy saucepan and heat, stirring as the butter melts, to a brisk boil. Lower the heat and gradually blend in the flour, stirring constantly. Continue stirring and cook until the mixture forms a ball, about 1 minute. Remove from the heat.

3. Add the eggs, one at a time, beating after each addition until well blended.

4. Drop the dough by teaspoonfuls onto the prepared baking sheet, about 3 inches apart. Bake for 20 minutes, lower the oven temperature to 350°F.; then bake until the puffs are a light golden brown, about 10 minutes. Remove to a wire rack to cool.

5. When the puffs are cool, cut each in half horizontally and fill each bottom half with a mound of Pastry Cream and replace each top half. *Or* cut a small gash in the side of each whole puff and fill by piping cream into each with a pastry tube. Dust the top of each puff with confectioners' sugar or garnish each with curls of orange rind.

Pastry Cream
1 cup milk
3 tablespoons all-purpose flour
½ cup plus 2 tablespoons sugar
Pinch of salt
2 egg yolks, lightly beaten
1 teaspoon vanilla extract

1. In a small heavy saucepan or the top of a double boiler over simmering water, heat the milk until just below the simmering point.

2. Combine the flour, sugar, and salt in a small mixing bowl; then gradually stir in the milk until well blended.

3. Pour this mixture back into the saucepan and stir over low heat until thick and smooth, about 5 minutes. Do not boil. Gradually stir in the beaten egg yolks and cook, stirring constantly, until the mixture thickens again, about 3 minutes.

4. Remove from heat and spoon the mixture into a bowl. Stir in the vanilla and allow to cool to room temperature, stirring occasionally. Cover and chill thoroughly before using.

Banana Cream Mash 1 very ripe banana with 1 tablespoon lemon juice. Blend into the cream at the cooling stage. Omit the vanilla.

Strawberry Cream Blend in ¼ cup strained strawberry or raspberry preserves at the cooling stage. Omit the vanilla.

Chocolate-Orange Cream Add 1 ounce unsweetened chocolate in step 1, combining thoroughly with the milk as the chocolate melts. Add 2 tablespoons more sugar to the dry ingredients in step 2. At the cooling stage, blend in ½ teaspoon grated orange rind and reduce the vanilla to ½ teaspoon.

Almond Cream Substitute almond extract for the vanilla and blend in ¼ cup toasted slivered almonds.

Mocha Cream Add 1 ounce unsweetened chocolate and 1 teaspoon instant coffee granules in step 1 and add 2 tablespoons more sugar to the dry ingredients in step 2. Reduce the vanilla to ½ teaspoon.

"The party proceeds whether you're ready or not—so you'd best be ready."
Elsa Maxwell

Chocolate-Liqueur-Dipped Fruits

4 ounces semisweet chocolate
2 tablespoons butter
1 teaspoon fruit-flavored liqueur
Seedless grapes, unhulled strawberries, tangerine sections, diagonally sliced firm ripe bananas, preserved ginger

1. Combine the chocolate and butter in the top of a double boiler over simmering water and put over low heat to melt. Stir well to blend thoroughly. Do not allow to simmer. Remove from heat and stir in the liqueur.

2. The fruit should be washed, thoroughly dried, and chilled. Insert a small wooden toothpick in the stem end of each piece of fruit.

3. Dip each piece into the chocolate mixture, allowing a bit of the colorful fruit to remain uncovered (tangerine sections and bananas should be completely covered). Hold the dipped piece over the pan for a few seconds to allow any excess chocolate to drip off.

4. Insert the ends of the toothpicks into the holes of an inverted wire mesh strainer to dry. Remove the toothpicks, cover, and refrigerate.

Note: During the dipping process, it may become necessary to reheat the chocolate slightly, as the chilled fruit may cool it off.

"There is no love sincerer than the love of food."
George Bernard Shaw

A CHAMPAGNE PARTY

•

FOR 25 TO 30

"Be bright and jovial among your guests tonight."
Shakespeare

MENU

Champagne Punch (page 161)

Smoked Salmon Mousse with Cucumber Slices

Veal and Ham Pâté

Fruits Wrapped in Smoked Turkey and Prosciutto

Scallop Rumaki   Caviar-Stuffed Eggs

Prairie Caviar with Tortilla Chips

Red Pepper Cheese with Melba Toasts

Aubergine Caviar with Endive

Raw Vegetables with Curried Cream

Strawberries with Pistachio Cream

Chocolate Praline Lace Cookies   Banana–Nut Cakes

*H*ere's the opportunity to pull out all the stops and throw an elegant, once-a-year party. When I'm having a New Year's Eve party, I like to send out printed invitations well in advance and ask everyone to dress to the nines. I also let everyone know there will be plenty to eat, so they can skip dinner beforehand if they want to.

This is a varied menu that's not difficult to prepare, and it

> "The log was burning brightly,
> 'Twas a night that should banish all sin,
> For the bells were ringing the Old Year out,
> And the New Year in."
>
> *Will Godwin*

should satisfy almost everyone's taste and appetite. I prefer to serve almost everything abundantly arranged on a lavish buffet table. Cute little hors d'oeuvres sparsely arranged on trays to be passed among the guests may look very pretty in pictures, but I find them a bit too precious and time consuming in real life. The passing trays constantly interrupt conversation and passers get in the way. With this buffet, guests can eat what and when they choose to (there is only one hors d'oeuvre to be passed, and that's only because it's hot). Just remember to keep an eye on the buffet table so that it's replenished when necessary and always looks neat and attractive.

Getting Ready: The food can be prepared at a leisurely pace; the only thing that needs to be done just before serving is the broiling of the Scallop Rumaki. But do leave yourself at least half an hour to arrange the table as spectacularly as possible just before the first guests arrive. The preparation countdown is as follows:

Up to 5 days ahead, make the Aubergine Caviar, the Red Pepper Mousse, Melba Toasts, and the Veal and Ham Pâté.

Up to 2 days ahead, make the Prairie Caviar and the Chocolate Lace Cookies, and boil the eggs for the Caviar-Stuffed Eggs.

The day before the party, make the Smoked Salmon Mousse, marinate the scallops for the rumaki, and make the Curried Cream for the vegetables and the Pistachio Cream for the strawberries.

On the day of the party, wash and separate the endive leaves to serve with the Aubergine Caviar, clean and cut up the raw vegetables and slice the cucumbers to be served with the Smoked Salmon Mousse; then store each individually wrapped in the refrigerator. Assemble the Scallop Rumaki and the Caviar-Stuffed Eggs. Cut up the fruit and assemble the Fruits Wrapped in Smoked Turkey and Prosciutto, and wash the strawberries to be served with the Pistachio Cream. Set up the coffeepot for the Anise Espresso and combine the chilled ingredients for the Champagne Punch just before the appointed hour.

Beverages: You could have an open bar here, but don't encourage drinking in excess. You could also serve straight Champagne in addition to the punch, especially at midnight to toast the new year. Be sure to have juices and sparkling waters available with a bowl of citrus fruit slices. Put out a pot of Anise Espresso just after midnight so everyone can have a cup or two before heading home, and replenish it when needed (it's easiest to keep two pots brewing).

Setting: I like to set the buffet table dramatically with a gold satin tablecloth, so the many colors of the foods stand out. Toward the back of the table I place a large round glass vase filled with an

188

arrangement of exotic white flowers and with gold and silver cords tied around it. Mismatched silver serving dishes and groupings of long white candles in crystal candlesticks add to the opulent effect.

For music, I try to make a tape every December of the preceding year's hits. And of course, without playing Guy Lombardo performing "Auld Lang Syne" it just wouldn't be New Year's Eve.

Smoked Salmon Mousse

MAKES ONE 4-CUP MOUSSE

1 tablespoon unflavored gelatin
¼ cup cold water
⅓ cup boiling water
⅓ cup sour cream
⅓ cup Homemade Mayonnaise (page 90)
1 small onion, very finely chopped
1 tablespoon lemon juice
3 tablespoons finely chopped dill
1 teaspoon salt
¼ teaspoon cayenne pepper
1 cup heavy cream
1¾ cups flaked poached salmon (or 1 15½-ounce can red salmon, picked over to remove skin and bones)
¼ pound smoked salmon, finely chopped

1. In a large mixing bowl, soften the gelatin in cold water, and let stand for 2 or 3 minutes. Gradually stir in the boiling water, and stir until the gelatin is dissolved. Refrigerate for 2 to 3 minutes, or until the mixture has cooled off.

2. Add all the remaining ingredients except the heavy cream and salmons and beat until well blended. Return to the refrigerator and chill about 15 minutes, or until the mixture is slightly thickened. (If the mixture becomes too thick, beat for a few seconds until smooth.)

3. While the above mixture is chilling, whip the cream in a separate chilled bowl. When the mixture has chilled and thickened, stir in the two salmons; then gently fold in the cream.

4. Oil a 4-cup mold and transfer the mousse to it, cover with plastic wrap and refrigerate until firm, at least 3 hours. To serve, unmold the mousse onto a platter and garnish with dill sprigs.

Spread this smoked salmon mousse onto thin cucumber slices or thin slices of dark grainy pumpernickel bread. If you've got two molds, you'd better make two mousses for a big party, because this always disappears quickly.

Veal and Ham Pâté

SERVES 12 AS A FIRST COURSE,

20 AS AN HORS D'OEUVRE

*T*his is a quick pâté to make as far as actual working time goes, but it needs to be started at least 2 days before serving. Make this in a ring mold and serve it with a crock of mustard in the center and surround it with small, thin slices of dark bread. This is a good recipe to double if you have two pans.

1 pound veal shoulder
¼ pound thickly sliced prosciutto or Westphalian ham
¼ teaspoon salt
½ teaspoon grated nutmeg
½ teaspoon ground allspice
½ teaspoon dried thyme
½ teaspoon dried basil
½ teaspoon freshly ground black pepper
1 medium onion, cut into eighths
3 large garlic cloves
¼ cup Marsala or Madeira
¼ cup dry red wine
¼ cup brandy
¼ cup fine dry bread crumbs
1 large egg, lightly beaten
1 pound bulk pork sausage
About 1 pound thinly sliced bacon

1. Cut the veal into small chunks and place them in a small shallow nonmetal bowl. Cut the ham into ¼-inch strips and place on top of the veal. Combine the salt, spices, herbs, onion, garlic, and liquors in a small bowl and pour over the meats. Cover and marinate overnight in the refrigerator.

2. Preheat the oven to 350°F. Remove the ham strips from the marinade and reserve. Remove the veal chunks, onion, and garlic to the bowl of a food processor fitted with a steel chopping blade and process until the meat is finely chopped.

3. Pour the marinade into a small skillet, place over high heat, and reduce by half.

4. Combine the veal mixture, reduced marinade, bread crumbs, egg, and sausage in a large mixing bowl and mix well with your hands until all the ingredients are very well blended.

5. Line a 4-cup ring pan or loaf pâté pan (preferably with collapsible sides) with bacon, overlapping the slices and allowing the ends of the bacon to overhang the sides of the pan. Patch any spaces in the lining with small strips of bacon.

6. Pack one-third of the pâté mixture in an even layer into the pan. Layer half of the reserved prosciutto lengthwise onto the pâté mixture. Repeat, and top with the remaining mixture. Cover the pâté with the overhanging ends of the bacon slices and patch any spaces with more bacon strips.

7. Cover the pan tightly with aluminum foil and place the pan in a larger baking pan filled with enough hot water to reach halfway up the sides of the pâté pan. Bake the pâté for 1 hour and 45 minutes.

8. Remove the pâté from the oven and allow it to cool to room temperature. Weight the top of the pâté (with filled cans or jars filled with water) and refrigerate for at least 1 day—2 days is better.

9. Unmold the pâté and serve with small thin slices of dark rye or pumpernickel bread and a crock of grainy mustard.

Fruit Wrapped in Smoked Turkey and Prosciutto

These fast and tasty hors d'oeuvres really require no formal recipe. Bread sticks and spears of Swiss or Jarlsberg work well, too. A pound of meat should yield about five dozen hors d'oeuvres.

Simply wrap ½ × 4-inch strips of thinly sliced smoked turkey or prosciutto around fresh fruit and arrange on a large platter garnished with flat dark green leaves. Some suggestions are:

With Prosciutto
Pineapple spears
Apple slices dipped in lemon juice
Spears of ripe cantaloupe or honedew melon
Quartered figs
Kiwi slices
Ripe pear slices dipped in lemon juice

With Smoked Turkey
Apple slices dipped in lemon juice
Peeled orange slices
Firm ripe peach slices
Ripe pear slices dipped in lemon juice
Halved hulled strawberries

Scallop Rumaki

I'm not a big fan of chicken livers, which are a usual ingredient in rumaki, hence this version using scallops. I also don't usually like serving anything with toothpicks (how many times have you come home from a cocktail party and discoverd a collection of picks in your pocket?), but these are so good, I'm making an exception. Marinate the scallops overnight, assemble the rumaki several hours ahead, and then pop them under the broiler about 10 minutes before serving.

Marinade
½ cup dark soy sauce
¼ cup firmly packed dark brown sugar
3 tablespoons finely chopped gingerroot
1 cinnamon stick
2 large garlic cloves, finely chopped
1 teaspoon dry mustard
2 scallions, white and green parts, finely chopped
½ cup orange juice

60 bay scallops (about 2 pounds)
20 thin slices bacon, cut in thirds
1 7-ounce can water chestnuts, drained and thinly sliced
Watercress

1. Combine all the marinade ingredients in a jar, cover, and shake well to combine all the ingredients. Place the scallops in a bowl, pour the marinade over them, cover, and marinate in the refrigerator for at least 3 hours, but preferably overnight.

2. To assemble, place a water chestnut slice on the center of each bacon slice and top with a scallop. Bring the edges of the bacon up over the scallop and secure with a toothpick. Cover well and refrigerate until half an hour before serving.

3. Preheat the broiler. Place the assembled rumaki on a rack in a broiling pan and place the pan about 4 inches below the heat source. Broil about 10 minutes, or until the bacon is browned and the scallops are opaque. Turn once during broiling to ensure the even browning of the bacon.

4. Arrange on a platter, garnish with watercress, and pass the platter immediately.

Caviar-Stuffed Eggs

MAKES 4 DOZEN

2 dozen hard-boiled medium eggs
¼ cup sour cream
¼ cup Homemade Mayonnaise (page 90)
¼ cup (½ stick) butter, melted and cooled
4 scallions, white parts only, finely chopped
3 tablespoons chopped fresh dill
Salt and cayenne pepper
2 ounces *each* red and black large-grained caviar
Dill sprigs
Several bunches watercress

1. Peel the eggs and cut them in half lengthwise. Scoop out the yolks and place them in the bowl of a food processor or a mixing bowl with the sour cream, mayonnaise, melted butter, scallions, and dill. Process or beat until the mixture is smooth. Season with salt and red cayenne pepper to taste (do not oversalt as the caviar is salty).

2. Transfer the mixture to a pastry bag fitted with the large star tip; then pipe the mixture into the halved egg whites. (The eggs may be made ahead to this point. Chill for about 10 minutes to firm up the filling; then cover loosely with aluminum foil or plastic wrap and store in the refrigerator until just before serving.)

3. Just before serving, use a tiny spoon to top each egg half with about ¼ teaspoon caviar; then garnish each with a tiny sprig of dill. Arrange the eggs in rows on a thick bed of watercress to prevent them from tipping. Alternate the rows of red- and black-topped eggs.

Prairie Caviar

MAKES ABOUT 6 CUPS

This inland version of a mock "caviar" combines two favorite flavors from the Deep South and the Southwest: black-eyed peas and jalapeño peppers. Black-eyed peas are, in fact, a Southern tradition for the new year, a legendary source of good luck. Serve Prairie Caviar with tortilla chips.

1 pound dried black-eyed peas
1 teaspoon salt
½ cup olive oil
¼ cup red wine vinegar
3 large garlic cloves
1 green pepper, finely chopped
1 red pepper, finely chopped
3 medium onions, finely chopped
5 to 6 scallions, white and green parts, finely chopped
4 jalapeño peppers, finely chopped

1. Pick over and wash the black-eyed peas. Rinse again and drain. Place the peas in a large pot, cover with water, add the salt, and place over high heat. Bring to a boil, remove from heat, cover, and let stand for 1 hour.

2. Bring the peas to a boil again; cover loosely, then boil until tender, about 15 minutes. Drain well; then remove 1½ cups of the peas to the bowl of a food processor fitted with a steel chopping blade. Add the oil, vinegar, and garlic, and puree until smooth.

3. Place the whole peas, pureed pea mixture, and the remaining ingredients in a medium mixing bowl and combine well. Cover and refrigerate overnight before serving. Serve in a lettuce-lined bowl.

Red Pepper Cheese

MAKES ABOUT 3 CUPS

An old Southern standby from my North Carolinian friend Ron Spainhour, this is good with crackers or Melba toasts as an hors d'oeuvre spread or between hot toasted slices of whole wheat bread as a sandwich filling.

1 pound sharp Cheddar cheese, grated
2 large red peppers, roasted and finely diced (page 90)
½ cup Homemade Mayonnaise (page 90)
¼ teaspoon cayenne pepper

Combine all the ingredients in a mixing bowl, cover, and refrigerate overnight before serving.

Aubergine Caviar

MAKES ABOUT 3 CUPS

This eggplant, or mock, "caviar" is wonderful served with endive leaves as edible scoops. It's good, too, with toasted thin slices of Italian or French bread or toasted quartered pita.

Melba Toasts

•

Homemade melba toasts are far better than store-bought and very easy to make. Preheat the oven to 300°F. Cut the crusts from thinly sliced white, pumpernickel, or whole wheat bread and cut each slice into quarters making triangles or strips. Or use cookie cutters to make decorative shapes, such as stars or hearts. Spread the bread on a baking sheet in one layer and bake for about 15 minutes, or until the bread is dry and just beginning to brown.

Cool the toasts on wire racks and store in tightly covered containers at room temperature up to 2 weeks.

1 cup finely diced celery
1 medium onion, finely chopped
¼ cup olive oil
3 cups peeled and diced eggplant (1 large eggplant)
3 tablespoons red wine vinegar
2 teaspoons sugar
½ cup tomato paste
4 teaspoons capers, rinsed and drained
10 large ripe black olives, pitted and chopped
1 tablespoon pignoli
2 tablespoons chopped parsley
Salt and freshly ground black pepper

1. Place the celery, onion, and olive oil in a large skillet and sauté over medium heat until the vegetables are crisp-tender, about 10 minutes. Remove the vegetables with a slotted spoon and set them aside.

2. Add the eggplant to the skillet, toss to coat with the oil, and sauté about 10 minutes, or until the eggplant is lightly golden. Add a tablespoon or so of olive oil, if necessary, to prevent sticking. Remove the eggplant with a slotted spoon and set it aside.

3. Add the vinegar, sugar, and tomato paste to the skillet and stir to combine all the ingredients. Bring to a boil, lower the heat, and simmer for 15 minutes.

4. Return the celery, onion, and eggplant to the skillet. Add the remaining ingredients, including salt and plenty of pepper to taste. Stir to combine, cover, and simmer about 15 minutes, or until the eggplant is very tender and the sauce is quite thick.

5. Cool; then transfer to a covered jar and store in the refrigerator. Will keep up to 10 days.

195

Raw Vegetables with Curried Cream

1 pint sour cream
1½ teaspoons curry powder
⅛ teaspoon ground coriander
⅛ teaspoon ground ginger
⅛ teaspoon cayenne pepper
¼ teaspoon salt
1 large garlic clove, finely chopped
2 scallions, white and green parts, finely chopped

1. Combine all the ingredients and mix thoroughly. Return the mixture to the sour cream container, cover, and refrigerate for several hours before serving.

2. Serve with any of the following vegetables: zucchini, carrot, and celery sticks; button mushrooms, or halved large mushrooms; cauliflower flowerets; cherry tomatoes and radishes; strips of red and green peppers; asparagus and snow peas, steamed for 1 minute; and broccoli flowerets and whole green beans, steamed for 3 minutes.

Strawberries with Pistachio Cream

1 pint sour cream
¼ cup firmly packed light brown sugar
½ cup chopped roasted red pistachios, shelled
¼ teaspoon vanilla extract
¼ teaspoon salt
2 quarts strawberries, washed but unhulled

1. Combine the sour cream, sugar, pistachios, vanilla, and salt, and mix well. Cover and refrigerate for several hours before serving.

2. Arrange the strawberries in a large shallow bowl and place a small bowl of the cream in the center.

Some people complain that crudités have become a cliché, but I've noticed that they are always one of the most popular nibbles at any cocktail party. I like to serve these on a large silver tray lined with big curly lettuce leaves, with a small lettuce-lined glass bowl of curried cream in the center.

Chocolate Praline Lace Cookies

MAKES ABOUT 4 DOZEN SANDWICH COOKIES

Pretty and delicate, these sandwich cookies are much easier to make than they look. Arrange a lavish display of them on a doily-lined silver tray for a buffet, or stand two cookies on either side of a scoop of rich vanilla ice cream in a crystal goblet for an elegant ending to a sit-down dinner. These cookies will keep up to a week, but are best served a day or two after they are made.

Cookies
1 cup (2 sticks) butter
1⅓ cups firmly packed light brown sugar
1 cup light corn syrup
1 teaspoon vanilla extract
3 tablespoons unsweetened cocoa powder
2 cups all-purpose flour
1 cup coarsely ground pecans

Frosting
2⅔ cups confectioners' sugar
¾ cup unsweetened cocoa powder
½ cup hot water
6 tablespoons Praline liqueur

1. Preheat the oven to 375°F. Grease baking sheets.

2. To make the cookies, melt the butter in a large heavy saucepan; then stir in the brown sugar, corn syrup, and vanilla. Bring the mixture to a simmer; then remove from heat.

3. In a mixing bowl, stir the cocoa powder, flour, and ground nuts together until thoroughly blended. Add this mixture to the contents of the saucepan and mix thoroughly to make a thick batter.

4. Drop the batter by scant teaspoonfuls onto the prepared baking sheets about 2½ inches apart. Bake about 5 minutes, or until the cookies have spread and the edges are browned. Do not overbake. Remove the cookies from the oven and allow them to cool for several minutes on the baking sheets before removing them to wire racks to cool further. Repeat until all the batter has been used.

5. While the cookies are cooling, prepare the frosting: combine the confectioners' sugar and cocoa powder and blend well. Slowly stir in the hot water to form a thick, smooth paste; then stir in the liqueur until well blended.

6. To assemble, spread a thin layer of frosting onto the flat bottom of a cooled cookie; then lay the flat side of a second cookie

197

onto the frosted side of the first one. Press gently to join. Store the cookies in a tightly covered container in a cool place; they will keep up to a week.

Chocolate–Almond Lace Cookies Substitute almond extract and almonds for the vanilla extract and pecans in the cookies; then use Amaretto for the Praline liqueur in the frosting.

Chocolate–Hazelnut Lace Cookies Substitute hazelnuts for the pecans and Frangelico for the Praline liqueur.

Mocha–Nut Lace Cookies Substitute walnuts for the pecans and Kahlua for the Praline liqueur.

Praline Baskets For a delicate container for dollops of Strawberry Mousse (page 159), follow the recipe for the cookies through step 2, but omit the cocoa powder. Drop the batter by *half* teaspoons onto the baking sheets and bake as directed in step 4. When the cookies are taken from the oven, immediately press them gently into lightly greased miniature muffin tins to form baskets and allow to cool.

Banana-Nut Cakes

MAKES ABOUT 4 DOZEN 1½-INCH SQUARES

⅔ cup vegetable shortening
2½ cups sifted cake flour
1⅔ cups sugar
1¼ teaspoons baking powder
1 teaspoon baking soda
1 teaspoon salt
1½ cups mashed very ripe bananas
⅔ cup buttermilk
2 large eggs
⅔ cup chopped walnuts

1. Preheat the oven to 350°F. Grease a 9 × 3-inch baking pan.

2. In a large mixing bowl, stir the shortening with a fork to soften it; then sift in the dry ingredients and mix well. Add the bananas and half of the buttermilk. Mix until all the dry ingredients are moistened; then beat vigorously for 2 minutes.

My mother always made this recipe as a layer cake, but I make it as a flat cake and cut it into bite-size squares. I had almost forgotten about this beloved cake from my childhood but discovered it again when I began going through my old recipe files in preparation for this book. I served the cake last New Year's to rave reviews. Thanks, Mom.

3. Add the remaining buttermilk and the eggs and beat for an additional 2 minutes. Fold in the nuts.

4. Pour the batter into the prepared pan and bake for 35 to 40 minutes, or until nicely browned and a toothpick or cake tester inserted in the center of the cake comes out clean. Cool the cake for 10 minutes in the pan; then remove to a wire rack to cool completely.

Frosting
1 cup sugar
¼ teaspoon cream of tartar
Pinch of salt
⅓ cup water
1 large egg white
¼ teaspoon vanilla extract
48 walnut halves

1. Combine the sugar, cream of tartar, salt, and water in a small heavy saucepan over medium heat. Stir well and bring to a boil; then remove from heat.

2. Slowly add the egg white, beating constantly with a rotary or electric beater. Continue beating until the mixture has reached a fluffy, spreadable consistency; then quickly beat in the vanilla.

3. Place the cooled cake on a cutting board and spread a thick layer of frosting over the top. Cut the cake into 1½-inch squares, and press a walnut half into the top of each square. Store the cake, covered, up to 3 days.

Anise Espresso

•

Here's a nonalcoholic alternative to espresso anisette, and a good pick-me-up for after dinner or before driving home. Crush 1 teaspoon anise seeds for every 4 cups of coffee by wrapping them in aluminum foil and banging them with a mallet. Add the crushed anise seeds and ¼ teaspoon grated lemon rind to the basket with the ground espresso beans before making the coffee. Serve in small cups with sugar on the side for those who like a sweetened espresso.

A ROMANTIC CANDLELIGHT DINNER

•

FOR 2

"One cannot think well, love well, or sleep well if one has not dined well."
Virginia Woolf

MENU

Champagne   Caviar with Melba Toasts (page 195)
Rack of Lamb with a Coat of Many Colors
Wild Rice with Morels   Sautéed Cherry Tomatoes
Green Salad with Red Hearts and Champagne Vinaigrette
Triple Crème Cheese and a Baguette
Champagne–Strawberry Sorbet
Chocolate–Hazelnut Truffles

*H*ere's a chance to get away from all the hustle and bustle of the season and share a quiet evening with That Certain Someone. This is a quick and easy menu to prepare—even so, why not cook it together, sipping Champagne all the way?

Getting Ready: The sorbet can be made up to a week ahead (the texture suffers if it's left in the freezer any longer), and the truffles can also be made well ahead and stored, tightly covered, in a cool place.

If the red pepper for the rack of lamb has been roasted early in

Caviar

•

Caviar, salt-preserved fish roe, comes from the sturgeon, salmon, carp, or whitefish. Traditionally, the best caviar has been from the Caspian Sea, but as the Iranian variety has become less available, there has been a great resurgence in the American caviar industry, at the mouth of the Columbia River in Oregon and in Lake Michigan. Some caviar types are as follows:

American Golden—from whitefish, is gold-colored, light in flavor.

American Black—this black sturgeon roe is more pungent than golden.

Salmon or Red Caviar—light orange in color and mild in flavor.

Pressed Caviar—is crushed roe, from the "bottom of the barrel."

Sevruga—from the sevruga sturgeon, with small black eggs and a somewhat mild flavor.

Beluga—known as the king of caviars from the Caspian Sea's beluga sturgeon; large gray or black eggs and a pungent flavor.

The best (and most expensive) way to serve caviar is in a small bowl on a bed of crushed ice, accompanied by Melba Toasts (page 195) and the classic condiments: finely chopped red onion, finely chopped eggs, and lemon wedges.

the day or even the day before, the "coat" takes less than 5 minutes to prepare in the food processor. As the lamb takes about 25 minutes to cook, start getting the coat ready about 30 minutes before serving.

Put the rice on to cook about 45 minutes before serving, and start sautéing the morels about 10 minutes before the rice is done. The cherry tomatoes literally take 5 minutes to sauté, so cook them just before serving.

The salad greens can be cleaned and torn and the vinaigrette mixed early in the day, or both can be prepared quickly just after putting on the rice. Dress the salad just before serving.

Buy the baguette and cheese when you do your marketing. The cheese should be taken out of the refrigerator about 30 minutes before serving. Warm the bread up in the already hot oven.

Beverages: There's no reason not to serve Champagne during the meal as well as before, but if you'd like a bolder wine with the lamb, try a medium-bodied red wine, such as a French Bordeaux or a California Cabernet Sauvignon. At the end of the meal, espresso with a chocolate liqueur goes nicely, or a simple snifter of Cognac.

Setting: I like to "put on the dog" with this dinner, making it that much more special. It's especially fun to dress formally for dinner, covering up with starchy white chef's aprons for the chores in the kitchen.

Set up a small table in the living room, or use just one end of your dining table. Use pale pink or snowy damask linens and set the table with floral-bordered china and your best silver. For the Champagne use your best crystal flutes, or if you don't already have them, plan a bit ahead and give a pair to your loved one as a special Christmas present. A few white sweetheart roses in a small crystal vase makes a simple, romantic statement. And don't forget candles on the table and all around the room in profusion—no electricity allowed!

For a musical background, put on whatever music is the most romantic to you, whether it's Bernstein conducting Brahms or Ella Fitzgerald singing the Harold Arlen Songbook—and don't forget to play "your song."

Rack of Lamb with a Coat of Many Colors

SERVES 2

A rack of lamb, perfectly roasted to a rosy pink, is one of life's true treats. I never really cared much for lamb until I learned that it could be cooked to be rare and juicy, and now it's one of my favorites. This is a rather expensive cut, but for a special occasion, it's well worth it. The pretty coating here enhances the flavor of the meat wonderfully without overpowering it.

1 small red pepper, roasted and peeled (page 90)
2 tablespoons butter, softened
1 tablespoon Dijon mustard
1 teaspoon lemon juice
1 teaspoon green peppercorns
2 small shallots
1 tablespoon fresh *or* 1 teaspoon dried rosemary leaves
½ cup loosely packed parsley
1 rack of lamb (7 chops), trimmed
Rosemary sprigs

1. Cut the red pepper into quarters and place them in the bowl of a food processor fitted with the steel chopping blade. Process until coarsely chopped in 3 or 4 quick pulses.

2. Add the butter, mustard, lemon juice, peppercorns, shallots, rosemary, and parsley. Process until the parsley is finely chopped and a coarse, rather dry paste has formed.

3. About 30 minutes before serving, preheat the oven to 500°F. Place the lamb on a rack in a small roasting pan, meaty side up. Put the pan in the upper center of the oven and roast about 10 minutes, or until the lamb is well seared.

4. Remove the pan from the oven and lower the oven temperature to 400°F. Using your hands, pat the paste onto the surface of the meat in a layer about ⅛ inch thick. Return the lamb to the oven and roast about 15 minutes more for medium-rare. If using a meat thermometer, the temperature should be 125°–130°F. Do not overcook.

5. To serve, carve the rack into individual chops. Place 2 to 3 chops on each serving plate and garnish each serving with a few sprigs of fresh rosemary.

Wild Rice with Morels

SERVES 2

¾ cup wild rice
2 cups water
½ teaspoon salt
¼ cup (½ stick) butter
12 to 15 small morels

1. Rinse the wild rice several times in cold running water, then pick over carefully to remove any foreign particles. Rinse again.

2. Bring 2 cups water and the salt to a boil in a medium heavy saucepan. Slowly add the rice, stir, cover, and bring to a simmer. Simmer the rice for 40 minutes, or until it is tender and all the water has been absorbed. Stir occasionally to prevent the rice from sticking and add a little more water if the original water is absorbed before the rice is tender.

3. While the wild rice is cooking, brush the morels very gently with a soft brush to remove all dirt particles. Melt the butter in a small skillet over medium heat; then add the morels. Sauté for about 10 minutes, or until the morels are quite tender and darkened.

4. Add the sautéed morels to the cooked rice and toss gently until the butter is blended into the rice. Season with plenty of freshly ground black pepper and serve hot.

Sautéed Cherry Tomatoes

SERVES 2

2 tablespoons olive oil *or* butter
½ pint cherry tomatoes, halved
¼ teaspoon dried basil *or* thyme
Salt and freshly ground black pepper

Place the olive oil or butter in a small heavy skillet and place over medium heat. Toss in the halved cherry tomatoes and a few pinches of dried basil or thyme. Sauté, tossing now and then, for 3 to 4 minutes, or until the tomatoes are just heated through. Season with salt and pepper to taste.

This is an earthy yet heavenly combination. Both the rice and the morels, intensely flavored wild mushrooms, cost about their weight in gold, but only small quantities of each are required here. (When I was a boy, we used to hunt morels in the woods right after the spring rains. Now, alas, I have to buy them.) If fresh morels are unavailable, substitute another variety of wild mushrooms, such as porcini or chanterelles. Or use dried wild mushrooms, plumped up by setting in warm water for about 10 minutes.

Green Salad with Red Hearts and Champagne Vinaigrette

SERVES 2

1 small red pepper
1 head Boston lettuce, washed and torn
2 tablespoons olive oil
2 tablespoons vegetable oil
2 tablespoons Champagne vinegar
1 teaspoon snipped chives
1 teaspoon Dijon mustard
Salt and freshly ground black pepper

1. To make red hearts, halve and seed the red pepper; then cut it into 1½-inch triangles. Trim off two of the corners of each triangle and cut a small V out of the center of the side between the trimmed corners.

2. Arrange the lettuce on two salad plates and top it with the red pepper hearts.

3. Combine the remaining ingredients in a small bottle or jar, cover, and shake well to combine. Drizzle the dressing over each serving.

Champagne-Strawberry Sorbet

MAKES ABOUT 1 PINT

2 cups strawberries
½ cup sugar
½ cup Champagne
Whole strawberries
Mint leaves

1. Wash and hull 2 cups strawberries and drain them well. Place the berries in the bowl of a food processor fitted with a metal chopping blade and puree.

"Drinking Stars"

•

Champagne, a symbol of extravagance and celebration, was born around 1670 in the wine cellars of the Hartvillers Abbey in the Champagne region of France, discovered by a young Benedictine monk, Dom Pierre Perignon. When he took his first sip, legend tells us, he exclaimed, "Look! I'm drinking stars."

France's king, Louis XIV, was a red wine drinker, so the effervescent amber Champagne conquered Britain before becoming popular in its homeland. Lost time was made up quickly in France, and Voltaire claimed that the bubbly wine was found in the soul of every Frenchman.

Champagne had reached its celebratory status by the time George Washington toasted the birth of the United States. America now has its own "Champagnes," some of them quite excellent, as well as being less expensive than the original. Cheers!

2. Combine the sugar and Champagne in a small saucepan over medium heat. Heat, stirring until the sugar has dissolved and small bubbles form in the bottom of the pan. Remove from heat and stir in the strawberry puree.

3. Pour the mixture into a small metal pan (a small square cake pan is ideal) and place in the freezer. When ice crystals begin to form, about 50 minutes, remove from the freezer and beat the mixture until smooth. Return the pan to the freezer and repeat this process two or three times, or until a smooth, firm, and finely grained consistency has been reached.

4. About 30 minutes before serving, remove the sorbet from the freezer to the refrigerator to allow it to soften slightly. At serving time, scoop into stemmed, wide-mouthed glasses. Garnish each serving with a whole, unhulled strawberry and a mint leaf.

Chocolate-Hazelnut Truffles

MAKES ABOUT 20

1½ pounds semisweet chocolate
½ cup heavy cream
3 tablespoons Grand Marnier *or* Frangelico liqueur
½ cup unsweetened cocoa powder
2 teaspoons ground cinnamon
About 20 whole hazelnuts, shelled

1. Melt the chocolate in the top of a double boiler over simmering water. Add the heavy cream and liqueur and stir until well blended. Cool the mixture to room temperature; then beat until fluffy. Chill until firm but pliable.

2. While the chocolate mixture is chilling, mix the cocoa powder and cinnamon together in a small bowl and set aside.

3. When the chocolate mixture is chilled, use your hands to form small balls about ¾ inch in diameter around the hazelnuts. Roll each ball in the cocoa-cinnamon mixture; then chill until firm. The truffles may be stored in a cool place in a tightly covered container for several weeks.

These classic confections are chocolaty, rich, and pure self-indulgence. They're easy to make, and they make wonderful gifts, too. Try varying the liqueur for a subtle difference in flavor.

"THE MORNING-AFTER" BUFFET BRUNCH

•

FOR 12

MENU

Bloodies (page 213) and Screwdrivers

Ham and Cheese in Puff Pastry

Confetti Home Fries

Grandma Wynn's Sautéed Apples

Warm Orange Gingerbread with Ginger Cream

Faye's Coffee Cake

This simple brunch offers one "comfort food" after another—just the thing for the morning after a late night out—and it's an easy meal to eat on laps, so you don't even have to set the table if you don't want to. If you're up to it, and New Year's morning turns out to be a chilly one, you might also want to serve the Mulled Wine Wassail Bowl on page 72.

Getting Ready: The Sautéed Apples, if made ahead and reheated, tend to get mushy, so prepare them just before serving.

The Bloody Mary mix can be prepared a day ahead and refrigerated. The Ham and Cheese in Puff Pastry can be assembled ahead and refrigerated, or even assembled well in advance and frozen, tightly wrapped. Just thaw for 1 hour in the refrigerator before baking.

If you're making the Confetti Home Fries ahead, undercook them slightly; then reheat in a skillet just before serving.

The Orange Gingerbread can be made a day or two ahead and stored, tightly covered, at room temperature. Warm it up in the oven, which should be turned off, but still fairly hot from baking the Ham and Cheese in Puff Pastry. It only takes a few minutes to whip the Ginger Cream just before serving.

Faye's Coffee Cake can be made a day ahead, if necessary, but is at its best when freshly baked, which doesn't take long at all.

Beverages: In addition to the Bloodies and Screwdrivers, you may want to serve Cranberry Mimosas (page 96) before eating and a good dry red jug wine or cold beer with the main course. That and a pot of hot coffee should do the trick.

Setting: Keep it simple; you've already done enough by getting up at the crack of noon and slaving over a hot stove. Put a cheery print cloth on the table along with a rustic basket filled with daisies, no fancy arrangement. Put out a stack of un-fancy plates and a mug filled with forks (no knives are needed) and a mug of spoons if you're serving coffee. Bloody mix, orange juice, and vodka can be set out in big pitchers, along with glasses and a bucket of ice, and each guest can mix his own. Serve the Ham and Cheese in Puff Pastry on a wood cutting board and the Sautéed Apples and Confetti Home Fries in bowls or right from the skillet.

"A drunken night makes a cloudy morning."
Sir William Cornwallis

"One of the reasons I don't drink is that I want to know when I am having a good time."
Lady Astor

Ham and Cheese in Puff Pastry

MAKES 24 FINGER SANDWICHES

These simple one-piece "sand-wiches" can be endlessly varied. Try prosciutto and pro-volone with a sprin-kling of chopped black olives, chorizo sausage and Monte-rey Jack cheese with chopped jalapeño, or Westphalian ham and Jarlsberg cheese. Store-bought frozen puff pastry makes preparation quick and easy, but if you must be a purist, make your own with your favorite recipe. These can be assem-bled ahead of time and refrigerated, then popped into the oven just before serving.

1 pound puff pastry
¼ cup grainy mustard
¾ pound thinly sliced Glazed Country Ham (see page 112)
¾ pound thinly sliced Cheddar or Swiss cheese
1 egg white, lightly beaten with 1 tablespoon water

1. If using frozen puff pastry, defrost in the refrigerator for 1 hour before using. Divide the pastry in half and roll half out onto a floured board into a rectangle approximately 12 × 16 inches. With a sharp, wet knife, cut the rectangle into two 12 × 8-inch rectangles.

2. Spread half of the mustard in a thin layer over one rectangle of pastry, leaving a ½-inch border on all four sides. Layer half of the ham evenly over the mustard, then half of the cheese over the ham.

3. Brush the uncovered pastry border with a bit of cold water; then place the unlayered rectangle of pastry on top. Press the edges together and crimp with your fingers as you would a pie. Prick the surface all over with a fork.

4. Preheat the oven to 400°F. Then repeat the assembly process using the remaining pastry, mustard, ham, and cheese. (This may be made ahead and refrigerated at this point.)

5. Brush the surfaces of the pastry with the egg white–water mixture to glaze. Place each pastry packet on an ungreased baking sheet and bake for 12 to 15 minutes, or until the pastry is puffed and golden brown.

6. Remove from the oven and allow to rest for 5 minutes. Care-fully transfer to cutting board(s) and cut each rectangle into twelve 2 × 4-inch rectangles. Serve immediately on the cutting board(s).

Confetti Home Fries

SERVES 10 TO 12

4 pounds boiling potatoes
½ cup (1 stick) butter *or* bacon fat *or* a mixture of both
2 garlic cloves, finely chopped
2 medium onions, chopped
1 medium green pepper, chopped
1 medium red pepper, chopped
¾ teaspoon paprika
Salt and freshly ground black pepper

1. Scrub the potatoes well and cut them into thin slices. Melt the butter and/or bacon fat in a large skillet over low heat and add the potatoes, garlic, onions, and peppers. Toss to coat all surfaces with fat.

2. Cover the pan and sauté, tossing occasionally, for about 30 minutes or until the potatoes are tender and nicely browned. Season to taste with paprika, salt, and pepper. Serve hot.

Grandma Wynn's Sautéed Apples

SERVES 12

½ cup (1 stick) butter
12 large tart apples, unpeeled, cored, and cut into ¼-inch rounds
3 tablespoons light brown sugar
1 teaspoon ground cinnamon
½ teaspoon grated nutmeg

1. Melt the butter in a large skillet over low heat; then add the apples to the skillet. Toss the apples to coat them with the butter; then cover and sauté, turning the apples occasionally, about 20 minutes, or until the apples are tender but not mushy.

2. Remove the cover from the pan and sprinkle on the brown sugar, cinnamon, and nutmeg. Toss to melt the sugar and coat apples evenly. Serve warm.

*W*henever my mother sent us out to the vegetable patch to dig up some potatoes and pick a few peppers, we could almost be sure that home fries were in the offing. These can be prepared ahead and warmed up just before serving.

*O*ne of my favorite childhood memories is that of staying at my grandmother's house and waking up to the spicy scent of apples being sautéed for breakfast. As a savory variation, try adding 1 chopped medium onion to the apples while sautéing.

Orange Gingerbread

MAKES ONE 9 × 12-INCH CAKE/SERVES 12

⅓ cup butter, melted
⅔ cup milk
1 cup dark molasses
1 large egg, lightly beaten
3 cups sifted all-purpose flour
½ teaspoon baking soda
2 teaspoons baking powder
½ teaspoon salt
1 tablespoon ground ginger
1 teaspoon ground cinnamon
½ teaspoon ground cloves
2 tablespoons grated orange rind

1. Preheat the oven to 350°F. Grease a flat 9 × 12-inch baking pan.

2. In a large mixing bowl, stir together the melted butter, milk, molasses, and beaten egg until well mixed.

3. In a separate bowl, sift together the flour, baking soda, baking powder, salt, and spices. Gradually add this mixture to the liquid mixture, stirring constantly until completely blended. Stir in the grated orange rind.

4. Pour the batter into the prepared pan and bake about 50 minutes, or until a knife inserted in the center comes out clean. Cool in the pan and serve warm, cut into twelve 3-inch squares.

Ginger Cream

MAKES ABOUT 2 CUPS

½ pint heavy cream
Pinch of salt
Pinch of cream of tartar
1 tablespoon finely chopped preserved ginger
1 tablespoon syrup from preserved ginger

1. Using a chilled bowl and chilled beaters, whip the cream with the salt and cream of tartar until stiff peaks form.

2. Gently fold in the chopped ginger and ginger syrup.

> "Had I but a penny in the world, thou shouldst have it for gingerbread."
> *Shakespeare*

210

Faye's Coffee Cake

MAKES ONE 9-INCH SQUARE CAKE

This recipe comes from Ken Sansone. He says it's been in his family for ages, but it's attributed to his mother's cousin, Faye Davis. I can't really tell you how many this cake will serve—Ken says he and his brother used to polish off a whole one themselves when they were kids. This quick-to-make cake is good any time of day, any time of the year.

Cake
1½ cups sifted all-purpose flour
3 teaspoons baking powder
¼ teaspoon salt
¾ cup granulated sugar
¼ cup vegetable shortening
1 egg
1 teaspoon vanilla extract
½ cup milk

Filling/Topping
1 cup firmly packed dark brown sugar
4 tablespoons all-purpose flour
4 teaspoons ground cinnamon
¼ cup (½ stick) butter, melted
1 cup coarsely chopped walnuts *or* pecans

1. Preheat the oven to 350°F. Lightly grease a 9-inch square cake pan.

2. In a large mixing bowl, sift together the flour, baking powder, and salt. In a separate bowl, cream the butter and sugar together; then beat in the egg. Beat in the dry mixture and then the vanilla and milk.

3. To make the filling/topping, combine all the ingredients in a bowl and mix until coarse crumbs are formed.

4. Spread half of the cake batter in an even layer in the bottom of the prepared pan; then sprinkle half of the filling/topping mixture over it. Spread the rest of the cake batter over this, and top with the remaining filling/topping mixture.

5. Bake for 25 to 30 minutes, or until a cake tester or toothpick inserted in the center comes out clean. When done, cool in the pan on a wire rack. Serve warm or at room temperature.

211

ROSE BOWL INDOOR TAILGATE PARTY

•

FOR 8 TO 10

MENU

Samantha's Fabulous Bloodies

Hot Buttered Popcorn

Czech Choucroute Garnie

Mashed Potatoes with Skins

Grilled Tomatoes

Apple Butter Spice Cake with Cream Cheese–Nut or Sour Cream Frosting

The Rose Bowl Parade and the Rose Bowl Game are a part of our New Year's Day tradition, but most of us have to be content with watching it all on television. This indoor tailgate party, with stick-to-the-ribs fare, lets us bring the festive spirit of a real tailgate party inside with us, making for a smooth, easy day with family and friends.

Start off with Bloodies and popcorn, and plan to serve the main course at half-time. Save dessert for the end of the game.

Getting Ready: There's very little last-minute preparation here. The Bloody mix can and should be made the day before serving, or even several days ahead. Make hot popcorn in an electric corn popper right in the room where everyone's watching the game.

The Czech Choucroute Garnie can also be made up to two days in advance, but if you want to make it the same day you can put it into the oven about an hour before the game starts and it will be ready at halftime.

The potatoes should be put on to boil about half an hour before serving, but they require very little watching. About 15 minutes before serving, begin preparing the Grilled Tomatoes.

The cake can be made ahead and stored overnight in the refrigerator. Bring to room temperature before serving.

Beverages: After the Bloodies and popcorn, switch to an assortment of chilled beers and canned sodas in a big tin bucket of ice with the main course. Also serve hot coffee in an insulated jug to carry out the outdoor theme and to keep it hot away from the kitchen.

Setting: Drape a bold plaid blanket over the table and casually arrange roses in beer steins or trophies. Use simple stoneware and set out red paper napkins and simple flatware for the buffet in a picnic basket.

Samantha's Fabulous Bloodies

MAKES ABOUT 30 DRINKS

2 46-ounce cans tomato juice
1 46-ounce can V-8 *or* Vegemato juice
⅓ cup freshly grated horseradish
¾ cup Worcestershire sauce
2 teaspoons freshly ground black pepper
1 tablespoon Tabasco sauce
Juice of 1 lemon
Juice of 1 lime
1 2-liter bottle vodka
Lemon and lime wedges
Celery stalks

1. Mix all the ingredients except vodka, lemon and lime wedges, and celery stalks together in a large jug. Refrigerate and allow to mellow overnight.

2. To serve, put out a bucket of ice, an iced decanter of vodka, and a pitcher of Bloody mix, along with a dish of lemon and lime wedges, a tumbler filled with celery sticks, and the pepper grinder. Let guests mix their own drinks.

*T*his version of the Bloody Mary is always a great eye-opener at Samantha Joseph's country weekends in Connecticut.

213

Czech Choucroute Garnie

SERVES 8 TO 10

¼ pound thickly sliced bacon, cut into 2-inch pieces
1 4-pound boneless beef rump roast
1 4-pound pork loin roast, boned and rolled
2 medium onions, sliced
3 garlic cloves, finely chopped
2 tart apples, peeled, cored, and chopped
2 carrots, thinly sliced
4 pounds sauerkraut (fresh or in plastic bags), drained and rinsed
10 whole black peppercorns
¼ cup firmly packed dark brown sugar
1 cup dark beer

1. Preheat the oven to 325°F.

2. In the bottom of a large Dutch oven, cook the bacon over medium heat until most of the fat has been rendered. Remove the bacon and reserve it. Remove all but 2 tablespoons of fat.

3. One at a time, place the roasts in the Dutch oven and brown them on all sides. Remove the roasts and reserve. Add the onions, garlic, apples, and carrots to the pot and sauté for 10 minutes, stirring occasionally. Add the sauerkraut, peppercorns, brown sugar, and beer. Stir, cover, and simmer for 5 minutes.

4. Add the roasts to the pot, spooning some of the sauerkraut mixture over them. Cover and place in the oven. Roast for 2½ to 3 hours, or until the meats are very tender. Stir and baste occasionally.

5. When done, remove the roasts from the pot and let rest for 10 to 15 minutes before slicing. If the sauerkraut is too juicy, place the Dutch oven over a high flame and, stirring constantly, boil off some of the liquid.

6. To serve, place alternating ¼-inch-thick slices of the roasts around a large platter. Heap sauerkraut in the center, garnished with the reserved bacon pieces.

When I was growing up, this dish was a New Year's tradition for good luck. Many European countries have a version of a braised sauerkraut and meat casserole, which in France is known as Choucroute Garnie, but this is the one handed down through the Czech branch of my family.

Mashed Potatoes with Skins

SERVES 8 TO 10

infully enriched with sour cream and flavored with sautéed onions, these potatoes need no gravy, but you may want to spoon some of the pan juices from the Choucroute Garnie over them when serving.

10 large potatoes
¼ cup (½ stick) butter, softened
1 large red onion, coarsely chopped
½ cup sour cream
1 large egg, lightly beaten
Salt and freshly ground black pepper

1. Scrub the potatoes well and then place them in a large pot with salted water to cover. Boil until tender, 20 to 25 minutes.

2. While the potatoes are cooking, melt the butter in a small skillet over low heat. Add the onion and sauté until transparent and tender, about 15 minutes. Combine the egg and sour cream together in a small mixing bowl.

3. When the potatoes are done, remove from the heat, drain; then transfer to the pot. Mash with a potato masher, leaving the potatoes slightly lumpy. Then fold in the sautéed onions and sour cream-egg mixture. Season with salt and plenty of pepper and serve.

Grilled Tomatoes

SERVES 8 TO 10

4 to 5 medium tomatoes
¼ cup (½ stick) butter
¼ cup grated Parmesan cheese
Dried thyme
Salt and freshly ground black pepper

1. Preheat the broiler.

2. Slice the tomatoes in half horizontally. Place the halves, cut side up, on a broiling pan. Dot the surface of each half with butter, a sprinkling of Parmesan cheese, a pinch of thyme, and salt and pepper to taste.

3. Place under the broiler and broil until the tops are bubbly and golden brown, about 7 to 10 minutes.

Apple Butter Spice Cake

MAKES ONE 9-INCH SQUARE CAKE

2½ cups all-purpose flour
2 cups firmly packed light brown sugar
1¼ teaspoons baking soda
1 teaspoon baking powder
½ teaspoon salt
1 teaspoon ground cinnamon
½ teaspoon *each* ground cloves, ground allspice, and grated nutmeg
1¾ cups apple butter
⅔ cup apple juice
1 cup dark raisins
Cream Cheese–Nut Frosting *or* Sour Cream Frosting
10 walnut halves

1. Preheat the oven to 350°F. Grease and flour two 9-inch square baking pans.

2. In a large mixing bowl, stir together the flour, sugar, baking soda, baking powder, salt, and spices until thoroughly blended.

This is a perfect way to enliven out-of-season tomatoes. Whenever I serve them, everyone always asks what the secret is. Well, the secret is that there is none!

This is a fragrant old-fashioned cake that my grandmother used to make for us when we came over to visit after school. She served it with big glasses of cold, fresh milk. I still love it as an adult, but with strong, hot coffee.

Beat in the apple butter and apple juice until well blended; then stir in the raisins.

3. Pour the batter into the prepared pans and bake until well browned and a knife inserted in the center comes out clean, 40 to 50 minutes. Invert the layers onto wire racks, remove the pans, and cool.

4. Spread the frosting onto one layer, top with the other layer, and frost the top and side of the cake. Garnish with walnut halves, arranged around the top of the cake.

Cream Cheese–Nut Frosting
½ cup (1 stick) butter, softened
8 ounces cream cheese, softened
1 teaspoon vanilla extract
3½ cups confectioners' sugar
1 teaspoon grated lemon rind
½ cup flaked coconut
¼ cup finely chopped walnuts

1. Beat the butter, cream cheese, and vanilla together until smooth. Gradually beat in the confectioners' sugar, about ½ cup at a time, and continue beating until smooth.

2. Add the lemon rind, coconut, and walnuts. Beat until blended.

Sour Cream Frosting
1½ cups granulated sugar
½ cup firmly packed light brown sugar
1 cup sour cream
¼ cup (½ stick) butter, softened
⅛ teaspoon salt
1 teaspoon vanilla extract

1. Combine all the ingredients except the vanilla in a medium heavy saucepan and place over medium heat. Cook the mixture, stirring constantly, until it begins to boil. Lower the heat and simmer about 5 minutes, or until the mixture just beings to form a thin thread dripped from a fork.

2. Remove the pan from the heat immediately and pour the mixture into a small mixing bowl. Allow to cool 10 minutes. Add the vanilla and beat the icing for 5 minutes, or until it has cooled to room temperature.

Black-Eyed Peas for Good Luck

•

In the South, black-eyed peas eaten on New Year's Day are considered a source of good luck throughout the rest of the year. Some people in the South mix their black-eyed peas with rice and call it hoppin' John. Lindsay Miller's grandmother, Alma Folkes of Richmond, Virginia, always fixed black-eyed peas this way:

Soak 1 pound black-eyed peas overnight in water to cover. Fry 1 pound bacon, and combine the bacon, bacon drippings (that's what makes the peas so good), peas, and their liquid in a pot and simmer slowly for at least an hour, the longer the better, as the peas get mushier and tasier; then serve 'em up with stewed tomatoes. Good luck!

BACK-ON-THE-DIET DINNER

•

F O R   4   T O   6

M E N U

Herbed Tomato Soup

Roasted Chicken Breasts with Garlic and Rosemary

Julienne of Carrots and Zucchini

Endive, Watercress, and Red Pepper Salad

Pears Poached in White Wine

*A*las, all good things must, and do, come to an end. The Christmas tree has to come down, all the decorations have to be packed up and stored away for another year, and we have to think about finding a way to get our belts to buckle again at the same hole they did way back in November. This simple, elegant dinner for the family helps end the season and puts us back on the track in style, and its easy preparation leaves time for those end-of-the-season chores.

Getting Ready: This menu requires very little time in the kitchen. The Herbed Tomato Soup can be made up to three days ahead and stored in the refrigerator. The Poached Pears are best prepared no more than a day in advance. The Chicken Breasts with Garlic and Rosemary are best if marinated overnight, but are still quite tasty if only allowed to marinate for a few hours. If you have a food processor, the carrots and zucchini can be julienned very quickly and require only about 10 minutes preparation time, start to finish. The salad, likewise, takes only a few minutes to prepare.

Beverages: A glass of a good, dry white wine might accompany dinner, or perhaps a white wine spritzer (equal parts of white wine

218

and seltzer or sparkling mineral water on the rocks with a twist of lime). If you're swearing off alcohol along with heavy food, try one of the citrus-flavored sparkling mineral waters.

Setting: As an early harbinger of spring, which is really not that far off, place a pretty glass vase on the table, filled with spring flowers, which are now available even in January. Make this family dinner special by using your best china, flatware, and crystal on a bare table, minimizing the laundry chores.

Menu Variations: Instead of the soup, you might try a strong, well-seasoned chicken broth with a few sliced mushrooms and chopped scallions. For the vegetables, substitute Oven-Braised Leeks (page 44) or the Brussels Sprouts and Carrots with Two Mustards (page 43) from the Thanksgiving Dinner, halving the recipe in both cases. Either the Apple–Ginger Sorbet (page 69) or the Champagne-Strawberry Sorbet (page 204) would make a nice, light finish to the meal.

Herbed Tomato Soup

SERVES 4 TO 6

2 tablespoons butter
½ cup diced celery
4 large shallots, minced
1 28-ounce can imported Italian plum tomatoes
2 tablespoons chopped fresh basil *or* 1 teaspoon dried basil
½ teaspoon dried oregano
1 teaspoon dried thyme
2 tablespoons chopped parsley
2 bay leaves
2 cups chicken stock
Salt and freshly ground black pepper

1. In a Dutch oven or large heavy saucepan, melt the butter over medium heat; then add the celery and shallots. Sauté for 7 to 10 minutes, or until the celery is tender.

2. Add the tomatoes, herbs, and chicken stock, bring to a boil, and simmer about 30 minutes. Remove from heat, and remove bay leaves.

3. Puree the soup in batches in a blender or food processor, leaving the soup slightly lumpy. Season with salt and fresh pepper and serve hot in small bowls or cups.

When I make pesto at the end of the summer with the surplus basil from my garden in the country, I freeze some in ice-cube trays so I have pesto cubes to perk up soups and stews all winter long. For this soup I frequently toss in a large pesto cube and eliminate the shallots and basil below, which results in a zestier soup. But the recipe as written here, though more subtle, is equally good.

Roasted Chicken Breasts with Garlic and Rosemary

SERVES 4 TO 6

2 tablespoons olive oil
¼ cup lemon juice
4 garlic cloves, finely chopped
1 tablespoon dried rosemary leaves
1 teaspoon freshly ground black pepper
4 whole small chicken breasts, halved and skinned
Thin lemon slices

1. Blend together all the ingredients except the chicken and lemon slices in a jar. Cover and shake well to blend.

2. Place the chicken in a shallow bowl, pour the marinade over it, and toss to coat well. Cover and refrigerate for several hours or overnight. Toss occasionally while the chicken is marinating.

3. Preheat the oven to 350°F. Remove the chicken from the refrigerator and arrange in a shallow aluminum foil–lined baking pan, bone side down. Press any remaining rosemary and garlic into the surface of the chicken.

4. Roast for 35 to 40 minutes, or until the chicken is firm and golden brown. Garnish each piece with a lemon slice, and grind fresh pepper over each before serving.

Julienne of Carrots and Zucchini

SERVES 4

1 tablespoon butter
2 tablespoons chicken stock
4 medium carrots, peeled and cut into ⅛-inch julienne
2 medium zucchini, unpeeled and cut into ⅛-inch julienne
½ teaspoon dried chervil
Salt and freshly ground black pepper

1. Melt the butter in a medium skillet over medium heat and stir in the chicken stock. Add the carrots, zucchini, and chervil and toss to coat the vegetables.

2. Cover the skillet and sauté about 5 minutes, or until the vegetables are crisp-tender, stirring occasionally. Season with salt and pepper to taste.

Pears Poached in White Wine

SERVES 4

½ cup orange juice
¾ cup fruity white wine
1 cinnamon stick
½ teaspoon whole allspice
½ teaspoon whole cloves
Zest of 1 orange
1 tablespoon lemon juice
4 medium firm ripe pears

1. Place all the ingredients except the pears in a small heavy saucepan just big enough to hold the 4 pears standing upright. Stir to blend and bring to a simmer over low heat.

2. While the poaching liquid is heating, carefully peel the pears, leaving the stems intact. When the liquid is simmering, dip the pears in it one at a time and toss to coat; then place them upright in the pan and cover.

3. Bring to a simmer again and simmer slowly for 15 to 20 minutes, or until the pears are just tender (test with a cake tester). Carefully remove the pears into individual serving dishes. Raise the heat and boil the poaching liquid down to about ¾ cup. Remove the spices and pour the liquid over the pears. Serve warm or chill thoroughly before serving.

I conjured up this recipe for real "down and dirty" dieting. It contains no sugar, allowing the sweetness of the pears to be complemented by the sweetness of the poaching liquid. If you're not dieting, however, top the pears with a dollop of whipped cream or crème fraîche and a sprinkling of chopped pecans.

INDEX